# Japanese Mythology

Mysteries and Wonders of Ancient Japan: Tales of Gods and Legendary Creatures

## Aula Magna

© **Copyright 2023 Aula Magna - All Rights Reserved**

The contents of this book may not be reproduced, duplicated or transmitted without the written permission of the author or publisher.

Under no circumstances shall any legal fault or liability be attributed to the publisher or author for damages, repairs, or monetary losses due to the information contained in this book, directly or indirectly.

**Legal notice**

This book is copyrighted. This book is for personal use only. You may not modify, distribute, sell, use, quote, or paraphrase any part, or the content within this book, without the consent of the author or publisher.

**Notice of disclaimer**

Please note that the information in this document is for educational and entertainment purposes only. Every effort has been made to present accurate, up-to-date and reliable, complete information. No warranty of any kind is stated or implied. Readers acknowledge that the author makes no commitment to provide legal, financial, medical, or professional advice.

# Table of Contents

Introduction: .................................................................. 3
Chapter 1: Ancient Mythology ............................... 5
Chapter 2: Sanctuaries ............................................ 10
Chapter 3: Pre-war power ....................................... 14
Chapter 4: TENGU: The Mountain goblin ........... 23
Chapter 5: KAPPA (also called KAWATARŌ) ...... 39
Chapter 6: TSUKUMOGAMI: The Yōkai Egg ....... 50
Chapter 7: AZUKI-ARAI: The Beans Washer ....... 57
Chapter 8: ZASHIKI-WARASHI ............................ 60
Chapter 9: YUKI-ONNA: The Winter Woman ..... 64
Chapter 10: KITSUNE: The Evanescent Fox ........ 70
Chapter 11: TANUKI: The Raccoon Dog ............... 80
Chapter 12: BAKENEKO: The Yōkai Cat .............. 85
Chapter 13: KASA-BAKE The Umbrella Yōkai ..... 90
Chapter 14: All Deities from A to Z ...................... 93
Conclusion ............................................................. 179

# Introduction

Few topics are as widely discussed in the Japanese studies community as Shintoism. As Japan's sole claim to a set of native traditions and mythologies that has changed and transformed over centuries and political conflicts, subsuming military power and outside influences, scholars have different perspectives on Shinto's status as a religion. The customs and folklore that make Shinto what it is have managed to penetrate almost every aspect of daily life in Japanese society. For this reason, many Japanese do not consider themselves religious, but rather participants in Shinto traditions, visiting shrines throughout the year. Therefore, scholars sometimes classify Shinto not as a religion but as a part of daily life.

The purpose of this book is to collect and report information on various aspects of Shinto as a whole, from its ancient mythology to its applications to the present day, and to provide snapshots of Shinto over the years to document the ways in which it has been influenced by the regional and international political climate. The mythology and traditions that have been passed down through the centuries are held in high regard and are well known throughout the nation. How is Shinto practiced in today's Japan?

What role have certain Shinto beliefs played in influencing Japanese institutions and government over time? What historical events may have influenced the way Shinto is viewed in society?

Let's find out together!

## Chapter 1

Ancient Mythology

Shinto is, at the most basic level, the indigenous religion of Japan, and its documented history dates to the 6th century, passing through many influences and various changes. It is mainly a set of beliefs centered on ancestor worship and the concept of sacred nature. Certain aspects of nature such as trees, forests and mountains are personified in the form of Kami, deities or spirits worshipped in sacred places throughout Japan.

Although these Kami can range from small spirits reigning over a single tree to powerful deities reigning over the entire sky, all receive the respect of those who visit Japanese shrines in the form of prayers, ablutions and offerings.

To learn more about Shinto and the kami developed within it, the best place to start is, of course, The Beginning: The Creation of the World. We can find information about Shinto in the Kojiki, the closest thing to a "sacred" book in the religion, and which illustrates a collection of ancient mythologies fused with historical facts. Originally, the paradises, which housed many latent spirits, were a vast dark sea.

Two twin kami, the male Izanagi-no-Mikoto and the female Izanami-no-Mikoto, took the paradises as an example to create life from the sea.

They descended from the clouds wielding bejeweled spears that they used to mix salt and clay with water. When they lifted them into the air, particles dripping from the blades piled up in the sea to form large islands, which would later become the land we know as Japan. From there, these two kami created a home on the first island, now known as Awaji Island, and erected a temple with the name Onokoro Shrine, considered by many to be the first shrine.

The two kami decided to marry in their temple, and then proceeded to give birth to the many spirits that would later become the lakes, forests, and all other aspects of nature on the islands.

Izanami died a horrible death because his body could not bear the birth of a fire spirit. In mourning, Izanagi made a journey to the underworld to try to bring her back to life.

But after seeing Izanami's decomposing zombie-like corpse, Izanagi fled the terrified Netherworld and immediately began to wash the impurities of death from her body into a nearby river. From the fallen drops of water, three new kami were born: Amaterasu Omikami, the powerful sun goddess; Susano-o-no-Mikoto, the brash and strong god of the seas; and Tsukuyomi-no-Mikoto, the peaceful moon god The first two became the protagonists of mythology.

This trio of kami children would later become the most revered among the vast number of Shinto kami worshipped in Japan. In particular, Amaterasu and Susano-Wo are known to be in constant disagreement, and many of their quarrels and squabbles caused problems for the other kami. One of the best-known stories in mythology is the one in which the sun hid. After a particularly bitter quarrel, the vengeful Susano-Wo decided that the best way to get back at his sister was to desecrate her sacred celestial weaving hall. While the goddess was weaving sacred robes with her damsels, Susano-Wo interrupted her peace by destroying the ceiling of the hall and dropping into the room the corpse of a dappled horse that had been skinned from tail to head.

This created a bloody mess inside the hall, ruining Amaterasu's woven robes, and at least one of her weaver damsels died from the surprise. Tired of her brother's aggressive behavior and disrespect, the goddess angrily fled and locked herself in a cave. Being a sun spirit, Amaterasu left the world without the light and warmth it needed to survive, causing chaos throughout the land. The other kami pondered what had to be done to bring the sun back into the sky and finally decided to try to lure Amaterasu out of the cave with the one thing they were certain he could never resist: a good party. Outside the cave, many kami gathered and made a great racket, with shouts and noises simulating a wild party, banging pots and singing.

One kami woman known as the goddess of merriment and revelry, Ame-no-Uzume-no-Mikoto, overturned a washstand, stripped off her clothes and began to dance on it, showing her breasts and intimacy. This provoked loud cheers and laughter from those present. Hearing a party to which she had not been invited, Amaterasu became jealous, wondering how everyone could be having such a good time without her, and finally came out of the cave to see what all the fuss was about. As she scanned the world, the first thing she laid eyes on was a large mirror that the other kami had hung on a tree branch, and she was immediately struck by its beauty. It came out enough for the other spirits to close the cave and force the sun to bring light back into the world, which came back to life.

# Chapter 2

Sanctuaries

Visiting the shrine is part of participation in Shintoism and plays a key role in the daily lives of many Japanese. It is not viewed in the same way, for example, as going to church on Sunday is viewed in Christianity, but rather represents a place of quiet reflection and, at the same time, noisy and turbulent celebration. In his research, John K. Nelson conducted surveys and interviews with visitors to Japanese shrines to understand what brings them closer to these ancient traditions in today's modern, fast-paced and technologically advanced age. Across the relatively small and densely populated island, there are about 80,000 shrines according to "official" estimates, and this does not take into account private shrines, shrines in homes, and neglected ancient shrines in the middle of forests or mountains. Because of this abundance, temples are seen as common places in everyday life, miniatures of which can even be found on suburban sidewalks and wedged between vending machines on street corners in busy cities. While the shrines themselves can vary widely depending on their location or purpose, most contain multiple key components that make them what they are. For example, the red-painted torii, which has become an unmistakable symbol of Shintoism as a whole, is a doorway at the entrance to the shrine and is typically seen as the gateway between the secular world and the sacred realm of the kami.

Just beyond the stone step, a small well overflows into a pool of water, and using the spoon hanging below, shrine visitors are invited to wipe their hands and mouths in a form of forgiveness, which purifies the body and soul before prayer. From there, the temple's administrative office, the Ema tablets ( there is a structure designed to hang handwritten wooden prayer boards), the worship hall with the donation boxes, the large hanging votive bells, the main hall that houses the kami, are all located somewhere on the same floor, and the location varies from shrine to shrine. Shinto itself, in the minds of the Japanese people, is simply a way of life they have grown up with, rather than a rigid system of religious belief they have chosen to follow. In this way, many Japanese people tend to identify themselves as not belonging to any religion while participating in Shinto tradition and ritual. Many of these people grew up visiting shrines for festivals throughout the year, for picnics during Hanami, or to pray for good health during the new years. Therefore, making the decision to participate in shrine activities is as natural and ordinary for these people as going to work or school.

Many times, visitors to certain shrines do not even know the kami that resides within them, as shown in a survey by Nelson: only 14 percent of visitors to temples on a given day know the name of the shrine's kami; one of the senior priests, not named by Nelson, was surprised by this: he expected the number of visitors who knew the name of the kami to be even lower.

Similarly, many of the activities practiced in shrines, such as praying, making offerings or making wishes are quite ingrained in daily life. While the idea of kami may be somewhat supernatural, the natural structure is very real and concrete, and many shrine-goers believe that the power of kami lies in the physical structure of what they represent.

Given the obvious religious behaviors, such as belief in gods and spirits and the perpetuation of ritual practice, perhaps some might wonder why some scholars are not inclined to label Shinto as a religion. As mentioned earlier, this is because nowadays an increasing number of Japanese consider themselves without religion, at least in the way religion would be described by the Western mindset. Compared to the large scale of other religious institutions such as the Catholic Church, Shinto does not claim a broadly structured institution; rather, the many shrines and places of worship are run independently by a few families or groups of priests with their own individual practices, beliefs, and local rules.

# Chapter 3

Pre-war Power

While many of these traditions and beliefs have remained remarkably unchanged over time, it should be noted that there has been a significant change in the role that Shintoism has played in Japanese society, particularly in the last century. From the 19th century and into the heart of the 20th century, Shinto beliefs were a driving factor in the growing Japanese ultranationalism that eventually led to the events of World War II. In a University of Tokyo article from just a century ago, Kitasawa describes the Shinto perspective as rooted in the main attachment to government, used as a source of propaganda to unite citizens daily under the belief that the emperor was a direct descendant of the sun goddess Amaterasu and that the Japanese race had the divine right to rule all. Kitasawa writes his article in English to share with foreigners an explanation of Shintoism, such as the importance of ancestor worship and filial piety, as well as purity and cleanliness in worship ritual. He places special emphasis on this idea of purity, explaining that shrines, human bodies, and even human souls are "characterized by simple rigidity" and should not be "allowed to be defiled." For believers like Kitasawa, their theology contains no concept of original sin and instead propagates a belief in the "innate goodness and divine purity of the human soul." This translates into a general love of cleanliness in the home and personal hygiene. At the end of his article, Kitasawa moves away from the precise description of Shinto beliefs and begins to reveal his personal beliefs in Japanese supremacy based on an "undivided loyalty" to the old deities. This was a common sentiment found in Shintoism in Japan during his time; the concept of Japanese supremacy, given by the popular belief of descent from the deities themselves, fueled the fire that led to some of the most heinous crimes in the history of World War II. In a journal article by Shimazono and Murphy, the two analyze in detail the four phases of Shintoism from the beginning of the Meiji Restoration in 1868 to the end of World War II in 1945.

The "Formative Period" (1868-1880) was a period of new beginnings for Japan, and propaganda focused on returning people to a more traditional era by restoring the emperor's power. This period was marked by the consolidation of palace rituals and the reorganization of all the shrines surrounding Ise Jingu, the main temple dedicated to Amaterasu.

The "doctrine completion" period (1880-1905) came next, and was initially defined by the revival of Shintoism as a national ritual system, as outlined in the Imperial Constitution.

The current doctrine referred specifically to the addition of Shinto belief (especially that which holds that the imperial family has divine origins) to the educational system as an ideological basis. A movement supported by the Imperial Rescript on Education.

This period culminated in the Russo-Japanese War. The third phase went down in history as the "system completion period" (1905-1930), from the end of the Meiji era to the Showa era, bringing with it an intense state interest in strengthening the relationship between government and religion as one and the same institution. The state increased control and economic support of shrines and mobilized temples as an ideological base, and this caused tensions between Shintoists and the many Buddhists spread throughout Japan. The final phase is known as "the period of fascist state religion" (1931-1945), in which the state had full control over the use of Shinto ideology as prewar propaganda. As Kitasawa's words suggest, many Japanese had already subscribed to the idea that their ethnicity was descended from the gods and therefore by its very nature superior to other peoples. This idea was essential to justify the Japanese invasions of Korea and China; it was an out-of-control religious ideology, and it was transmitted by the government to the people as a justification for the horrific atrocities committed during World War II.

Post-war calm

As the world began to pick up the pieces after the war, there was an immediate change in the role Shinto played in Japanese society. The changes that the United States urged in the Japanese constitution were reflected in this religious institution. On January 1, 1949, Emperor Showa declared, "The ties between the United States and our people have always been based on mutual trust and affection. They do not depend on mere legends and myths. Their lives are not based on the false notion that the emperor is divine and that the Japanese are superior to other races and destined to dominate the world." While this statement shocked those who had subscribed to this belief of superiority, the transition from a state-publicized religion to an independently functioning structure was rapid, thanks to the ever-watchful eye of the United States. In the modern postwar period, Shimazono writes about the state of the religious structure in present-day Japan, analyzing in detail how many Japanese were "uncomfortable" with the concept of religion, and this corresponds to the rapid decrease in those who call themselves religious. "State Shinto," i.e., government-established Shinto, was abolished under the new constitution and was replaced by "Shinto Shrine," treated by the government as a "religious institution for the people" that requires freedom of belief and allows for the development of various organizations.

From myth to movement

It is not unusual for tales from ancient mythology to influence the practices of the time, and Shinto is no stranger to this. For example, at the beginning of the tale of Susano-Wo's revenge, Amaterasu creates the sacred robes of the gods with her maidens inside her sacred weaving hall, an action that is believed to have been passed down through the centuries in the form of two festivals held in the center of the temple dedicated to Amaterasu, Ise Jingu: the spring and autumn Kammiso-sai, or "festival of the robes of the gods."

These biennial festivals, characterized by the creation of sacred robes made of a special fabric, ended with eight women weavers presenting the robes to Amaterasu as an offering, accompanied by all the gestures of a classical sacred ritual such as bowing, kneeling, clapping hands, and reciting the norito or words of the sacred ritual. Although these ideologies were taken from an extremely small section of mythology, entire rituals grew out of it, filled with symbolism and devotion to the goddess with an attempt to offer her new sacred robes because hers had been desecrated.

A second ritual practice is also believed to be derived from this particular myth. Ame-no-Uzume-no-Mikoto, the goddess of merriment previously named for helping to lead the sun goddess out of the cave in the tale of Amaterasu's hermit refuge, and her wild dance have been recognized as the core of a traditional ritual dance called kagura, often performed by the Miko (temple maids).

Ame-no-Uzume-no-Mikoto itself is considered the origin of 'asobi,' a term used to describe both traditional entertainers, especially singers and dancers of low social status, and the form of entertainment they practice.

The world asobi comes from the Japanese verb 遊ぶ [asobu] meaning 'to play,' and this is exactly what these entertainers are trained to do. As entertainers, they are expected to perform not only for their followers but, following in the footsteps of Ame-no-Uzume herself, also spiritually for Amaterasu.

Mythology, however, is not the only source of these spirit-based traditions, and sometimes the traditions themselves also have an effect on social conventions. Shinto holds in high regard the beauty of the natural world, for example, ancient forests and mountains, as kami, and a reflection of this can be found in a place many people would not expect: the garbage dump. Japan has one of the strictest regulations in the world regarding recycling and the separation and depositing of various types of waste.

This is largely due to the traditional view of the importance of cleanliness, both physical and spiritual, as seen in the need for purification fountains in shrines, as well as the need to reduce waste in the interest of environmental well-being. The Japanese often spend time separating their waste so that each piece can be fully recycled, even going so far as to separate plastic wrapping and caps from bottles and discard them separately.

As history shows, the concepts and applications of Shinto have changed to fit the nature of Japanese society over time. From its beginnings as a ritualistic and animistic ancestor cult, to its structure of Buddhist influence as a religious institution, to its status as a vessel of nationalist extremism in the early 20th century, to its passive existence in the contemporary world, Shinto has been changed according to influences both within Japan and outside, in the world at large. Regardless of the form it takes, Shinto is one of Japan's innate institutions, dating back to the ancient tradition of the "age of the gods," and has exerted a strong authority over them, as if trapped in time, in a Japan that is nonetheless constantly evolving and modernizing. The island nation has managed to project its ancient narratives into the future by creating a diverse and mixed social environment that embraces both aspects of its culture. Shinto has maintained a sense of identity for the Japanese-for better or worse-but it has never had a deeper influence in Japan's rapidly digitizing scenario, simply representing a shrine to the memory of the beauty, magic, and power of the natural world around us.

# Chapter 4

TENGU: The Mountain Goblin

One of the best-known yōkai ever, the tengu has long played a changing role in Japanese history, religion, literature, and tradition. Often depicted as a "mountain sprite," tengu tend to have bird-like features and superlative martial arts skills. They are often associated with Buddhism and ascetic mountain practices. Even today there are mountain shrines and festivals that honor tengu.

There are two types of tengu. The first is the karasu tengu, literally a 'raven tengu,' a bird-like creature with wings, a beak and the ability to fly. Despite the word crow, karasu tengu are often portrayed as prayer birds, particularly tonbi (kites). During the Edo period, the karasu tengu was gradually replaced by a more human-looking creature, tall, dressed like a Buddhist monk or another practiced religion, and characterized by a long, rounded, red nose. This long-nosed tengu is the most commonly depicted version in Japanese culture to date. In some cases, karasu tengu are portrayed as owners of this illustrious long-nosed image of theirs.

Tengu literally means "celestial dog" or "divine hound" (Chinese: tian gou) and the same combination of ideograms is found in various ancient Chinese texts, referring to a comet or star or perhaps a "huge dog-shaped meteorite."

In Japan, the word is first found in the Nihonshoki, early in the year 637, where it is documented that "a great star sailed from east to west and there was a noise similar to that of thunder." A monk explains that this is not a shooting star, but rather a "celestial dog, whose barking is like that of lightning."

Despite the continued use of the ideogram "dog," later references to the tengu never really depict it in its appearance or behavior as a dog. Instead, it is almost always depicted as anthropomorphic and/or avian.

It is impossible to reconstruct the exact process by which a word, initially translatable as "divine hound" and indicating an astronomical event, is gradually transformed and mispronounced to become "a monk with a long nose and wings," but it is clear that this transformation reflects a mixture of historical, religious, and folk influences. For example, the avian image of the tengu might be associated in some way with Garuda, a divine bird figure that plays an important role in Hindu and Buddhist beliefs, which most likely entered Japan through China, predating Buddhism itself. But just as Buddhism went through many changes in its long journey across continents, so the tengu, along with the meanings and images associated with it, changed with different historical circumstances.

During the Heian period, tengu were thought to be mysterious forces residing in the mountains. Similar to mono-no-ke, they were amorphous evil spirits that could cause disease or war or could torment an individual. There are some accounts of how they could appear during this period: generally, they were invisible, but occasionally they could appear in the form of a bird or a monk. It was not until the Kamakura period that the tengu really began to acquire more definite characteristics. Considered the embodiment of emperors or dead warriors, they appeared as evil bird-like creatures, monks or yamabushi ("mountain ascetics"), descending from the mountains to torment those in power.

In the Taiheiki (Chronicle of the Great Peace; late 14th century) Emperor Sutoku, exiled to an isolated region, is described plotting together with a group of demons and tengu the best way to destroy humankind. It was also during this period that the tengu cultivated a deeper relationship with Buddhism. In particular they were associated with the concept of ma, the devil who hinders a person on the path to enlightenment.

Some setsuwa collected stories in the late Heian period of tengu possessing and teaching supernatural powers called gejutsu (external techniques): non-Buddhist magic that was deceptive and could be used for evil purposes. Although tengu might appear to be experienced monks, in reality their powers were false and would not lead to enlightenment. But like many yōkai, they are ambiguous. In one tale, for example, a mountain ascetic was summoned to heal a sick emperor. He demonstrated magnificent magical powers by quickly curing the emperor, but his priests, having studied the way of the Buddha, were suspicious of the ascetic's mysterious abilities and began sending him spells. Immediately the ascetic rushed out of his tent and fell to the ground, lying flat on his back. "Help!" he cried. "Kind lords, save me, please! All these years on the Kōzen I have worshipped the tengu and begged them to make me famous. And it worked, you know, because I was called here to the palace! But what a terrible mistake that was! Now I have learned my lesson, of course I have learned it! Please save me, oh, please!"

Although the ascetic had followed the tengu's fake path to fame, his healing of the emperor seemed genuine. Although the power of tengu may not agree with Buddhism and may never lead to enlightenment, in this example at least, it still proves effective. A concept called Tengu-dō, the Way of Tengu, developed during this period: "a realm reserved for practitioners of Buddhism who had failed to overcome the temptation of evil." A text called Hirasan kojin reitaku, for example, documents an evocative dialogue between a monk and a tengu. The tengu, speaking through a young woman he had possessed, told the monk about the otherworldly realm of Tengu-dō and its inhabitants. With refined zoological details, he also described the tengu themselves as beings as tall as ten-year-old children, with human bodies and heads, short tails, bird-like legs, and wings about a meter long. In disputes between different Buddhist temples and sects, one faction could sometimes slander the priests of another sect by pointing them out as tengu.

Representing a monk from an opposing temple as a tengu was a way of demonizing him and indicated that his teaching was dangerous and deceptive.

Tengu, Yoshitsune and the warrior arts.

At the same time, we can also imagine how tengu could become powerful symbols of the dispossessed by representing a rebellious and anti-authoritarian spirit. It is perhaps in this context that they became famous as masters of secret martial arts techniques. The most famous legend is that the tengu trained Minamoto-no-Yoshitune, one of the greatest warriors in Japanese history.

Yoshitsune was the younger brother of Minamoto-no-Yoritomo, the leader of the victorious Genji forces in the Genpei War (1180-1185), the great civil conflict that led to the founding of the Kamakura government. As general of the Genji, Yoshitsune was famous for his military prowess, which, according to legend, he learned from the tengu when he lived as a child in Kurama Temple in present-day Kyoto. This explanation of his military prowess seems to have become part of cultural and folk beliefs fairly early on.

In the Kamakura period Heiji monogatari (The Tale of Heiji), for example, simply notes that "it is said that Yoshitsune, night after night, was instructed in the martial arts by a tengu in Kurama-yama. This was the reason why he could run and jump beyond the limits of human power."

The relationship between the tengu and Yoshitsune, or Ushiwaka, as he was called as a child, was reworked in a Noh work, Kurama tengu, and in a lesser-known dramatic-literal form, called kōwakamai, from the Muromachi period. The latter work, titled Miraiki (Chronicle of the Future), begins with Ushiwaka practicing every evening in a wooded area behind the Kurama temple. Some tengu noticed him and at first took offense at his intrusion into their territory. But when they recognized that he was training to avenge his father's death, one tengu said to the other, "We are known as tengu, there is a reason for that. Long ago we were human, but by studying the dharma well we felt that there was no one more competent than us, and because we were puffed up with pride, we failed to become Buddhas and fell into the Way of the Tengu. But even though this pride caused our downfall, there is no reason why we should not feel pity. So let us help

Ushiwaka, let us teach him the Way of Tengu so that he can attack his father's enemies."

And so, appearing to him as yamabushi, the tengu invited Ushiwaka to their abode. Ushiwaka was suspicious of these monk-like figures, but feeling brave, he agreed to accompany them. He was soon taken to a mountain he had never seen before, a beautiful place with dense forest, majestic rocks, the scent of flowers and the sound of waterfalls.

They entered a magnificent temple, where a hundred tengu played musical instruments. Ushiwaka joined them for a delicious lunch filled with food from the mountains and rivers, flavored with all kinds of spices.

The tengu (who presumably still appear as monks or yamabushi) then proceeded to put on a kind of show, in which one by one they took on the roles of key characters in the Genpei conflict for which Ushiwaka was training. In essence, they recited the future for him, explaining his role in the conflict and informing him that after the last battle he would fall out of favor with his older brother.

All their predictions, of course, were accurate: in fact, the reader or observer of the Chronicles of the Future already knows that Yoshitsune ends up being atrociously killed by his older brother. Interestingly, in any case, there is no explicit training described in the story; perhaps simply receiving this vision of the future is enough to make Ushiwaka a superior warrior. When the tengu finished their performance, they gave the boy a small iron ball as a token of their visit and then disappeared. Immediately Ushiwaka found himself on a branch of a pine tree behind the temple. He thought, "Well, I have been deceived by the tengu."

The tengu here, and also in the Noh work, are usually portrayed as generous creatures eager to assist Ushiwaka in his struggle for justice; here we see the more cooperative side of their character. Whether or not this reflects a general change in the tengu's approach is difficult to ascertain, but it clearly demonstrates the tengu's deep involvement with the human world.

Mysterious disappearances

During the Edo period, the figure of the tengu evolved into that of a monk with a long nose and wings for which they are known today, a change in their representation that scholars are still unable to clearly explain. Perhaps one reason for this change, however, was their growing identification with humans and the workings of humanity, as if the tengu kingdom were a strange mirror of the human world. Indeed, reflecting the highly structured society of Tokugawa-period Japan, the tengu were hierarchically ordered: the long-nosed tengu called daitengu (large tengu), flanked by a group of bird-like tengu karasu called kotengu (small tengu).

In addition, during this period the tengu became increasingly associated with mountain worship and deeply integrated into all forms of local traditional beliefs.

They were often invoked to explain mysterious events. The sound of a tree falling in the forest, for example, could be attributed to the plots of a tengu called tengu-daoshi (tree-felling tengu). A loud snickering that echoed throughout the forest was called tengu-warai (tengu laughter).

At other times the tengu could cause real damage. At a certain place in the city of Gifu, for example, a tengu is said to have built his home in a large pine tree. If a fisherman wanted to go fishing nearby, the tengu would throw stones at him to persuade him to reconsider. And if that did not stop him, the tengu would capsize his boat.

More famously and frighteningly, tengu were often responsible for something called kamikakushi: abduction by a god, which can be translated as "mysterious disappearance," or more literally, "hidden by a deity." The details of these events vary, but usually the story goes like this: a young man or teenager suddenly disappears. His family and villagers frantically search for him but to no avail. Then, some time later, he finds himself in a strange place -- in a tree, or in the gutters of a house -- dazed but strangely unharmed. Sometimes he is able to tell of being abducted by a stranger, usually an older man, who has taken him to faraway places.

A story from Takayama, Gifu province, for example, tells of a boy employed by a merchant family. The boy receives a new pair of geta (wooden sandals) from his boss and plans to wear them that night. However, his boss warns him that if he wears his new geta in the evening, "a tengu will take him away." But the boy is so excited about having the new shoes that he wears them anyway and sneaks out into the street-and no one sees him anymore.

When his master realizes that he is missing, a big commotion ensues and a group of people are recruited to search. Eventually, after about a week, they find the boy standing on a bridge, looking exhausted. He explains that that evening he was walking with his new geta, a big man with a big nose and wings on his back approached him and said, "Get on my back and I will take you to a nice place." The boy did as he was told, but he remembered nothing afterward. "The last thing I remember is when I realized I was on this bridge." The story ends with the comment, "They say he was a tengu."

Similarly, Yanagita Kunio documents an incident in 1877 in the city of Kanazawa, Ishikawa Province, related to a childhood memory of writer Tokuda Shūsei (1871-1943). In the house next to Tokuda's, a young man in his 20s disappeared under a large persimmon tree, leaving only his geta. After searching for a long time, everyone immediately heard a loud noise in the attic, as if someone had fallen down. When Tokuda's older brother went to investigate, he discovered the boy lying there. After carrying him downstairs, they saw that his mouth was green, as if he had been chewing on tree leaves.

When he had recovered sufficiently, he explained that a big man had come and taken him away; they had traveled here and there, eating wherever they were. After a while, he told the man that he had to leave and tried to escape-and this had happened when they found him in the attic.

There is, in fact, no specific mention of a tengu in this account, and certainly there must have been cases in the news where children were accidentally lost or killed or kidnapped by other humans. Although several yōkai (including kitsune and oni) may be implicated in these abductions, at least since the Kamura period tengu have been the most commonly accused perpetrators of these kinds of crimes. The legend of Ushiwaka mentioned earlier, for example, coincides with this pattern.

Even in the modern period, the correlation between this type of abduction and supernatural powers is clear. Yanagita tells another story from 1907, of a boy who disappeared during a festival in which the villagers made rice offerings to the deities. When the boy was found in the attic of a house, he explained that an old man had taken him from house to house to feast on the food offered to him, which is why his mouth was covered with rice. Again, there is no explicit mention of tengu, but it is clear that the boy was in the company of a supernatural being; we can also detect obvious similarities with the legend of Tokuda Shūsei.

Perhaps the most famous example of supernatural abduction during the Edo period is the story of Torakichi, a boy who claimed to have been taken on a series of mystical journeys around the world, and even to the moon, by an experienced tengu.

His adventures attracted the attention of nativist scholar Hirata Atsutane, who interviewed him and recorded his findings in a text called Senkyō ibun (Strange News from the Realm of Immortals). Although the text was steeped in Atsutane's particular religious and political perspectives, it reveals both fantastic and mundane details about the residents of the Underworld, including animals (real and legendary) and all sorts of demons.

In contemporary Japan, the idea of kamikakushi is still well known, mainly due to the great success of Miyazaki Hayao's manga Sen to Chihiro no kamikakushi (2001), correctly translated into English as Spirited Away. Although no tengu appears in the film, and the way the main characters "mysteriously disappear" is very different from the legends described here, the film's success at the box office exhumed the concept of kamikakushi in the popular imagination. Recently, it has been featured in literature and visual art and also as a theme for many websites.

At the same time, in contemporary Japan, tengu are often invoked as symbols of local identity while retaining their mysticism or historical associations.

In the city of Hachiōji, west of central Tokyo, for example, Mount Takao has many tengu statues, tributes to the legends associated with them in the area. And at the Takao-san Yakuō-in temple on the mountain, there are statues of long-nosed daitengu and beak-nosed kotengu. Rightly, the association of tengu with shugendō is still very active: the temple is a prayer center for mountain ascetics, where practitioners still undergo such labors as waterfall training and walking on hot coals.

The tengu's image and name are also commonly used in marketing. There is a popular chain of cheap izakaya (restaurant-bars) called Tengu, for example, which uses stylized images of long noses as its icon. There is also a famous sake made in Ishikawa province called Tengumai (tengu dance). In short, tengu have a long history, and although they have undergone many changes, they remain one of Japan's most distinctive and vital yōkai today, with roles in local community life, religion, tourism, and trade.

## Chapter 5

KAPPA (also called KAWATARŌ)

Kappa is associated with water, usually rivers, ponds or swamps. It is one of the most famous yōkai in all of Japan.

Various legends and beliefs about it are distributed throughout the country, but in general the kappa is thought to be scaly or slimy, greenish in color, with webbed feet and hands and a carapace on its back. Sometimes it resembles a monkey, other times a giant frog or turtle. It has the size of a small child but is disproportionately strong.

A concave indentation or hollow section on the kappa's head contains water, and if this water is spilled, the creature loses its incredible strength. Kappas are harmful and sometimes deadly, famous for drawing bears and livestock into the water. They are also known for drowning young children and extracting their internal organs from their anus.

Despite these bloodthirsty inclinations, the kappa can also be playful and sometimes overly honest. It especially enjoys sumo wrestling and challenges with passersby. The kappa is a dangerous monster and demon, a water spirit, and its figure is often used to warn children when swimming in a river or pond. One tactic for beating a kappa in sumo wrestling is simply to bow at first: when the kappa bends in response, he pours the liquid that gives him power from the hollow on his head.

Chinese tradition certainly influenced its development, but while similar water creatures exist everywhere in world folklore, the kappa, as described here, is considered a purely Japanese creation.

They are fond of certain foods such as melons, eggplants, and especially cucumbers. In many places, children are warned not to enter the water after eating cucumbers because they might be attacked by a kappa. In some communities, there is a tradition of leaving cucumbers in shrines or water as an offering to appease the kappa that resides there.

In addition, in Japan and many other parts of the world, sushi rolls made with cucumbers are called kappa maki, from the love kappa have for this summer vegetable.

Many local rituals and festivals, particularly in farming communities that depend on water for irrigation, celebrate kappa as water deities (suijin). If treated properly, the local kappa will provide abundant water, but if neglected or treated with disregard it will cause droughts or floods. The kappa, therefore, can be considered simultaneously a deity and a demon, depending on the viewpoint of the human being with whom it is in contact.

Kappa vs. Kawatarō

Scholars have collected images of kappa in different regions, essentially dividing the country into east and west. The shell-bearing creature, the amphibious yōkai, was generally found in eastern Japan, from the Kanto region to Tohoku. In western Japan, from Kansai to parts of Shikoku and Kyushu, the creature was called kawatarō (or some variation of this name), was hairy and walked on two feet like monkeys. It is no coincidence, for example, that the "kawatarō" in the Three Kingdoms above looks more like a monkey; the author, Terajima Ryōan, was from Osaka in the west of the country.

Similarly, a 1754 text called Nihon sankai meibutsu zue shows that a group of kawatarō from Bungo (today's Ōita province) in Kyushu walked on two feet and played by the river; the text describes them as "as large as a five-year-old child and with hair all over their bodies." In 1776, when Toriyama Sekien created an image entitled "Kappa, also called kawatarō," he carefully and perhaps consciously merged the name and image of the Western kawatarō with the name and image of the Eastern kappa. In later years, from the late 19th century and early 20th century, this generic version of the amphibious, slimy creature called kappa became the yōkai we know today.

Characteristics of the Kappa

With this complex history of regional variations and creative interactions in mind, we can identify a number of widely known characteristics of the kappa. As mentioned above, kappa are, for example, extremely fond of cucumbers. On the other hand, they are averse to certain materials, such as iron, an aversion common to many water spirits around the world. Their inability to deal with gourds, as demonstrated in the passage from the Nihonshoki quoted earlier, also persists in the later folkloric narrative known as 'Kappa muko-iri' (tale of the kappa groom). A farmer offered to give his daughter to anyone who could successfully irrigate his fields. He assumed this would be a human being, of course, but it was a local kappa who finally succeeded and received his daughter's hand. The bride-to-be understandably was not happy about the marriage, and challenged the kappa to sink the gourds into the river. Unable to complete this impossible task, the kappa grew tired and gave up on the marriage.

In the northern part of Japan, in particular, kappa were known to lure horses into the water: in some regions they are called komahiki, or "horse pullers." This nasty inclination to drown horses, and sometimes livestock, is balanced by the fact that, in many narratives, the kappa fail.

When the attempt fails the kappa, or just his arm, is dragged by the frightened horse to the stable. In this helpless condition, the kappa is open to negotiation with humans, and to regain his freedom or his arm, he will often promise, for example, to stop tormenting passersby, to help with field work, or perhaps to teach secret medicines and techniques for putting bones back together.

Kappa knowledge of medicine is a theme throughout Japan. In some cases, the negotiation of an ancestor with a captive kappa is touted as the origin of the lineage of a medical family. A legend from Ehime province reflects not only this secret medical knowledge, but also another terrible habit of the kappa. Long ago, the maid of a doctor's family went to the toilet at night, and out of the toilet she touched a hairy hand, perhaps a human or perhaps a monkey. She did not know what it was, and the creature made to caress her buttocks, but the maid ran away frightened and told her experience to the doctor.

Hearing this, the doctor grabbed a sword, exclaimed, "I'm going to defeat this thing," and entered the outside bathroom. When a hand came out of the bathroom, the doctor took it and cut it with his sword, with a sure and swift movement. He took the hand home to his laboratory.

The next evening, the doctor heard a knock at the front door and, thinking it was a patient, went outside and found that it was the Enko whose hand he had cut off the day before. "Doctor," said the Enko, "please give me back my hand. If I don't put medicine on it and reattach it quickly, I won't be able to do it anymore. I won't do anything wrong anymore," he apologized, "so please give me back my arm."

When the doctor initially refused, Enko signed an oath promising to teach him a remedy to repair the bones, so he was able to get his arm back.

Later, the doctor is said to have made his fortune as a specialist in bone repair.

Kappa's interest in fondling human buttocks is related to another, more ambiguous trait: his desire for an organ called shirikodama. The shirikodama is like a ball placed at the opening of the anus; if your shirikodama is torn off by a kappa, you will die. Of course, biologically speaking, there is no such organ, but one explanation for this belief is that the bodies of lured victims have an "open anus," as if something had been removed. In some cases, it is said that the target of kappa is not the shirikodama itself, but the internal organs beyond it.

Modern Kappa

Despite their potentially ambiguous and disgusting behavior, kappa have developed in modern Japan. They have been gradually rehabilitated, domesticated, and are often used in national advertising campaigns and local tourism promotion. This process of domestication certainly began with the comical appearance of the kappa in kibyōshi and other forms in the Edo period. In the 20th century, the creature made a particularly famous literary appearance as the protagonist of Akutagawa Ryūnosuke's short story Kappa (1927), a social satire narrated by a human traveling in the land of the kappa. In his depiction of the kappa characters, with their similarities and differences with humans, the author sharply criticizes certain aspects of modern Japanese society. Akutugawa was already quite famous when he wrote Kappa; his suicide shortly after publication drew attention to the satirical content and kappa characters of his last novel.

The appearance of kappa also developed in the 20th century. The artist Ogawa Usen (1868-1938), for example, was famous for his illustration of kappa playing merrily. As in Akutagawa's novel, kappas become stand-ins for humans. This is similarly clear in the popular comic strip by Shimizu Kon (1912-1974), whose Kappa tengoku (kappa paradise), along with the female kappa (rare in tradition) and the "employed" kappa (nonexistent in folklore), began nationwide circulation in the Ashai Weekly in 1953. Kojima Kō (b. 1928) also illustrated a nude female kappa with pink nipples and thick eyelashes, resembling a human except for the shell-like structures and flat blue disk located on the head. Images by both of these artists were used in advertising campaigns, most commonly those of Kizakura's taste.

In 1960, Mizuki Shigeru published a serialized comic strip entitled Sanpei the Kappa. The role of the Kappa as a national icon can also be seen in its use as a good luck charm for the DC Card (a credit card). In this case, the Kappa is associated with another popular yōkai, the tanuki.

Commercial use of the kappa can also be found locally. In the 1970s and 1980s, when many people were moving to cities, rural communities throughout Japan began to develop the local kappa tradition for the "village revival" project.

Celebrating the kappa's association with agriculture and the rapidly disappearing rural lifestyle, communities nostalgically defined themselves as traditional towns, attracting tourists and selling items based on these images.

Similarly, this slimy creature that once terrorized people and animals venturing near water has now become a symbol of unspoiled nature. One can find images of kappa lounging near rivers, imploring people not to pollute or ruin the environment. In other words, a yōkai that represented the violence and unpredictability of the natural world, especially water, has now literally become an emblem of the effort to stop the sacrifice of nature.

Kappas continue to appear nationally and internationally in popular media, especially in movies. Mizuki Shigeru's 1960s manga Kappa no Sanpei was revived as an animated series in 1990, and a kappa character had a starring role in E.T.'s Kappa (1994). The beginning of the 21st century has already seen many films about kappa, such as Yōkai daisensō directed by Miike Takashi (The Great Yōkai War, 2005); Desu kappa (Kappa Mort, dir. Haraguchi Tomo, 2010), featuring a kappa who transforms into a mammoth and tramples the city of Tokyo; and Imaoka Shinji's Onna no Kappa (2011, English title: Underwater Love), an erotic fantasy musical. Kappa remains a vibrant and versatile character, more than the satirical, if not frightening, commentary on human society.

Eventually, as one of the most recognized yōkai, the kappa also appeared internationally, in the famous Harry Potter and the Prisoner of Azkaban (1999) and in Rowling's bestiary Fantastic Animals and Where to Find Them (2001). Although this figure is not specifically celebrated as a mutant, he shows that he is very capable of adapting to all kinds of environments. After his humble beginnings as a foul sea creature in a Japanese river, he has now traveled the world.

# Chapter 6

TSUKUMOGAMI: The Yōkai Egg

Tsukumogami is a general term referring to all kinds of household utensils, musical instruments, and other man-made objects that have become yōkai. Tsukumogami-ki, an otogizōshi tale from the Muromachi period, explains that "when an object reaches one hundred years of age, it is transformed, obtaining a spirit (seirei) and deceiving people's hearts; this is called tsukumogami."

A related set of 16th-century scrolls from a temple in Gifu Prefecture also warns that there are tools and other objects that become spirits after a period of one hundred years and often deceive people. These spirits are called Tsukumogami. "At the end of the year, families discard old furniture and utensils and pile them on the side of the road. Then in the new year-when it is time to renew the hearth and draw new water-the clothes, household utensils and other items change. They get angry at the extravagant wealth of families. These tsukumogami should be treated with caution."

These scrolls offer a Buddhist salvation story, following a group of discarded utensils on their journey for revenge against humans. Eventually, the transformed objects are converted to the Buddha's way and they themselves finally attain the state of Buddhahood.

From the Muromachi period, if not before, there seemed to be a belief that objects not treated with respect, or thrown away improperly, could come alive and seek revenge against the humans responsible. As in many yōkai-related beliefs, the number one hundred seems to be central to this transformation. The word Tsukumogami itself may derive from a complicated wordplay associated with the number: Tsukumogami is read in the same way as tsukumo-gami 九十九髪, in which case the ideogram stands for tsukumo 九十九 (denoting the number ninety-nine), and gami (kami 髪) (denoting hair). The phrase, therefore, can be translated as "ninety-nine hairs" and would refer to the white hair of a woman in old age, in general. (The number ninety-nine is, of course, less than one hundred; the character of "white," i.e. 白 is similar to a short character stroke of one hundred 百, so it connects with whiteness.) Kami, meaning "hair," is also the namesake of the deities. The numbers here are not necessarily meant to be exact; both ninety-nine and one hundred may simply indicate that a very long time has passed, with the assumption that when a normal thing exists long enough, it can turn into something not so normal. An old tanuki might develop unpleasant magical powers, an old cat might become a bakeneko, an old human might become an oni, and even old objects might mutate into yōkai.

This animation process may reflect an animist worldview in which everything, including inanimate objects, potentially possesses a spirit. The transformation of things into yōkai represents the essence of what it means to be a bakemono, or a changing thing. As Komatsu points out, one of the most interesting aspects of the tsukumogami scrolls seen earlier is that the ultimate goal of each object's transformation is to mutate into a real oni. The scrolls that illustrate the process of this transformation describe the objects by mentioning the development of facial features, arms, and legs.

If becoming an oni is the goal of the transformation, then the tsukumogami, at least in this example, are stuck in the middle, no longer objects, but not yet oni. They are adolescent monsters, so to speak, stuck in the middle of transformation.

The fact that tsukumo is associated with the number ninety-nine adds the implication that these objects have almost, but not quite, completed their metamorphosis.

Just as the animate nature of all things suggests an animistic understanding of the world, so too does the potential for transformation reflect a Buddhist perspective in which there is always the possibility, in theory, of becoming a Buddha. In the case of tsukumogami, whether the object becomes a benign kami or an evil yōkai depends on how humans treat it: whether they respect it or, conversely, throw it in the trash. Even today in

Japan, memorial ceremonies (kuyō) are practiced for certain objects, particularly household utensils such as brooms, brushes, needles, dolls, and spectacles that have devoted their "lives" to helping men. To some extent, this attitude reflects a kind of ecological sensitivity, perhaps born of necessity, where nothing must be taken for granted. It may also reflect an economic and practical perspective where increased consumption of goods has been simplified by the ritual management of 'disposal of used and worn out objects.'

In popular culture, certain ideas about inanimate/animated objects provide an entertaining subject and the potential for social critique. The first famous images of tsukumogami appear in the cheerful emaki Hyakkiyagyō of the Muromachi period, but the idea has been reinvented several times in the modern period. An early 20th-century version, for example, frivolously reflects a particular anxiety of the time: a procession of tsukumogami candles, lanterns, and flashlights fleeing in frantic terror from a new and frighteningly powerful yōkai object in the form of an electric light bulb. It is equally easy to imagine a version of the early 21st century, full of discarded, wide-eyed computers and cell phones nagging at our every step.

# Chapter 7

AZUKI-ARAI: The Beans Washer

Azuki-arai is a yōkai that produces the sound of azuki (or adzuki) beans being washed into a river, lake or well. The phenomenon can be found in most of Japan, although the name may vary from region to region. For example, in parts of Okayama prefecture, it is called azuki-suri and azuki-sarasara, in a village in Yamanashi prefecture it is called azuki-sogi, and in parts of Nagano city it is called azuki-goshagosha. Along with the rinsing sound, chanting can sometimes be heard. Similar rinsing sounds have also been attributed to tanuki, kitsune, kawauso, and mujina.

While the origin of azuki-arai can be attributed to the sound of water flowing through pebbles and leaves, the connection to azuki is equally important. In Japan, azuki (Phaseolus angularis) and other beans are symbolically powerful.

During the Setsubun celebration at the beginning of February, for example, family members in many parts of Japan throw soybeans, shouting "out with the oni, in with the luck!" and then each person eats as many beans as their years. The magical properties of beans ward off evil and bring good luck for the following year. Similarly, special events such as weddings, graduations and other milestones are often celebrated by eating seki-han, rice cooked with red azuki beans.

Although the popular phenomenon of azuki-arai described above was acoustic, at least until the Edo period, a visual image was also associated with it. In an 1841 picture book of scary tales by Takehara Shunsen, for example, there is a story of a disabled Buddhist follower who plays, and is extremely skilled at counting beans. One day, an evil monk throws him into a well, and later his spirit appears at dusk and he can be heard rinsing and counting beans. The narrative is illustrated with an image of a clumsy man with a crazy smile and a demonic glint in his eyes, his hands inside a pile of beans. Mizuki Shigeru's image of azuki-arai is clearly based on this, and another further developed character appears in The Great Yōkai War (2005).

Azuki-arai is also an alternative name for chatate-mushi (literally, "tea-making insect," Psocoptera), a family of insects known to make noise at night in the shoji partitions of houses. The noise they make is said to be similar to that of making tea (cha or tateru) or, as it were, the rinsing of beans.

# Chapter 8

ZASHIKI-WARASHI: The Homes's Spirit

Zashiki-warashi are the yokai most associated with the Tohoku region of northeastern Japan, particularly Iwate Prefecture. Literally translated, the name means "living room child" or "little man of the house"; and as a result, zashiki-warashi reside just inside the house.

They usually resemble a child between the ages of three and thirteen, but there are also examples of zashiki-warashi women. There are many variations and regional names for this yōkai, such as zashiki-bokko, heya-bokko, kura-warashi, and kome-tsuki-warashi.

Not every house has a zashiki-warashi, but it is said that if one occupies a house, the family will prosper. If, on the other hand, one leaves the residence, the fortune will decrease. The zashiki-warashi generally refuse to be seen directly by the family, but rather, do harm in any way that is unnoticeable: knocking over pillows while people are sleeping, pulling blankets off the bed, making noise throughout the house. If the resident zashiki-warashi suddenly appears, this could be considered a sign of its imminent departure and a premonitory sign that the house will have to endure hard times.

One zashiki-warashi recorded in Aomori Prefecture was said to resemble a young girl who wore a red chanchanko (a sleeveless kimono dress) and turned visitors' pillows. She was considered a "protective spirit" (mamorigami) of the house.

In his famous collection Tōno (in Iwate Prefecture), Yanagita Kunio reported many tales about zashiki-warashi:

Kizen Sasaki's mother was sewing alone one day when she heard a light rustling in the next room. That room was only for the landlord, but he was in Tokyo. Thinking this was strange, she opened the door and looked in, but there was no one there. He sat down for a brief moment, but this time he heard the sound of someone sniffing in the next room. He concluded that it must be a Zashikiwarashi. There was noise for as long as the Zashikiwarashi resided in that house [sic]. It is said that a house in which this kami (spirit) lives becomes rich and prestigious.

In some cases, the Zashikiwarashi can be linked to the practice of mabiki, or infanticide, which was used to control the population in parts of rural Japan during the 18th century. An infant was not necessarily considered a real human being, so the dead infant was not to be commemorated in the traditional way. Instead, for example, the body was to be buried in the house itself, where it was thought there might be a protective spirit.

Although this interpretation of zashikiwarashi is speculative, it is clear that with one less mouth to feed, the house in question would have been a little more prosperous than before-exactly the effect that zashiki-warashi is said to bring.

Although zashiki-warashi are most commonly associated with the Tohoku region, similar yōkai or house-protecting spirits are found everywhere, much like ainukaisei in Hokkaido and akagantā in Okinawa.

## Chapter 9

YUKI-ONNA: The Winter Woman

The yuki-onna is a yōkai that appears on snowy evenings or in the middle of a snowstorm.

Specific names, beliefs and narratives vary from region to region. In Miyagi Prefecture, for example, she is called yuki-banba; in parts of Nagano Prefecture, she is known as shikkenken; in Yamagata Prefecture yuki-jorō; in Miyazaki Prefecture and the Satsuma region of Kagoshima Prefecture, she is known as yuki-bajo (bajo is the local term for "old woman").

In Iwate and Miyagi prefectures in northern Japan, it was said that if someone saw a yuki-woman, her spirit would be extracted from her body. In some parts of Aomori prefecture, her behavior is similar to that of ubume: she will ask you to hold her baby. In some parts of the country, such as Tōno in Iwate prefecture, she appears on a fixed date; elsewhere her appearance is random and witnessed only by particularly lucky, or unlucky, individuals. She is variously described as the spirit of snow, as the ghost of a woman who died in the snow, or even, in Yamagata prefecture, as a moon princess who has been cast out of the celestial world and comes down dancing with the snow. In one form or another, the yuki-onna seems to be common throughout the country. Toriyama Sekien includes it in his first catalog, along with the other yōkai for which no explanation was necessary.

Even with this wide distribution throughout Japan, yuki-onna is probably best known today thanks to a story written in English by Lafcadio Hearn in his 1904 Kwaidan; translated into Japanese, it was widely read throughout the last century. Hearn explains in the preface that the narrator of the yuki woman he tells was told to him "by a farmer from Chōfu, Nishitama-gōri, in Musashi Province, as a legend from his native village." One night, two woodcutters were caught in a terrible snowstorm and took refuge in a hut. The younger of the two, Minokichi, sees a beautiful woman dressed in white blowing smoke into his older companion's face, a cold breath that, he later discovers, takes the old man's life. The mysterious white woman then bends down to blow on Minokichi's face, but pulls back at the last second, leaving him alive, but with the warning that she will kill him if he ever reveals what he saw that night.

The following year, Minokichi meets a beautiful young woman named O-Yuki. The two soon marry and lead a happy and fruitful life together with their ten children. One night, however, Minokichi looks at his woman and, lost in his dream, tells her about his meeting with Yuki-woman many years before. At that instant, his wife becomes enraged and screams, "For those children sleeping there, I would kill you right now!" and with that she dissolves into a bright white mist that swells from the rafters and shudders through the smoke.

Although Hearn attributes the narrative to a local farmer, scholars have doubted this claim because its fully developed love story is significantly more complex than any other known local legend concerning yuki women. Indeed, Hearn himself had mentioned the simplicity of these legends much earlier, in an 1893 letter to Basil Hall Chamberlain: "Even Japanese fantasy," he wrote, "has its 'snow women.' Its spectres and sprites, which do no harm and say nothing, but frighten and make one feel cold." It is therefore possible that Hearn combined a simple Japanese legend with more complex and stylized European literary images of the 'femme fatale.' One scholar suggests that he was specifically influenced by Charles Baudelaire's poem 'Les Bienfaits de la Lune' (Blessings of the Moon).

Hearn's story of the yuki woman also incorporates a variety of folkloric themes, particularly the notion of marriage between humans and nonhumans. Common among these tales is the end of marriage when the husband, often accidentally, breaks a promise and the wife returns to her true form. In Japan, this theme appears as early as Kojiki and Nihonshoki; it is found in the widely used legends "Hagoromo" (Feathered Mantle) and "Tsuru-nyōbo" (Crane Wife), and there are numerous examples of men who married kitsune. The theme is also common in the folklore of other cultures, such as the Gaelic legends of the selkie. Many different sources influenced the development of her narrative, an evocative literary narrative that created an image that survives to this day, in Japan and abroad, as the most resonant image of the snow woman.

# Chapter 10

KITSUNE: The Evanescent Fox

The kitsune, or fox, is one of Japan's most famous yōkai; and perhaps more than any other it has also fascinated people outside the country. Although kitsune is the most common generic term for this yōkai, fox-like creatures are also known by several regional names, including ninko, osaki-gitsune, kuda-gitsune, and nogitsune.

The kitsune has many talents and appears in local culture, historical documents, literary texts, plays, and contemporary popular culture. It can be a dangerous mutant and can possess people; but it is also a classical element of Inari worship, and stone statues of kitsune are placed in shrines throughout the country. With all these different incarnations and meanings, it is fair to say that in Japan today the kitsune, a charming and cunning seductress who exudes an aura of danger and evil, is admired, adored and feared.

Many ancient Japanese tales about kitsune can be traced back to China, where the creatures were also known for their mutant gifts, most famously taking the form of beautiful and seductive women. Some of these stories were told in other literary genres and came to Japan in written texts. In China, the word huli, a combination of the ideogram of kitsune and tanuki, generally denotes a fox; in Japan the same compound of ideograms, pronounced kori, refers to all sorts of supernatural and disturbing events.

In Japan, kitsune and tanuki are both known for their ability to change shape and deceive others. The tanuki tends to be funny and less skilled in deception; the kitsune appears more serious in its performance, and its skills are better honed. Both creatures are members of the family Canidae. The folkloric characteristics of the kitsune, like those of the tanuki, reflect its zoological traits as a creature that can live on the fringes of human society, visible one moment and missing the next. The most common fox in Japan is the red fox (Vulpes vulpes), which is also "the most widespread carnivore in the world."

Kitsune are mentioned in early Japanese texts, such as the Nihonshoki, in which they appear as both good and bad omens. But they also turned into beautiful women and have attracted men since at least the ninth century, when one such story was recorded in a setsuwa collected in Miraculous Stories. A man met a beautiful and sensitive girl, married her, and they had a child. Around the same time, their dog gave birth to a puppy who persisted in barking at his wife. One day it frightened her: "terrified, she immediately turned into a wild fox and jumped over the edge."

Eventually the couple was forced to separate, but their love remained strong, and the wife came every night to sleep with the man, and from this, the text explains, comes the word kitsune: come (kitsu) and sleep (ne).

The etymology offered here is not generally taken seriously today; similar tales of faithful fox-women are found in history throughout Japan, some more embellished than others. One of the Tales of Old Times is particularly elaborate. It was the year 896 and a man named Kaya no Yoshifuji, who lived in Ashimori village in Bitchū province, was left to his own devices when his "wife" went to the capital, leaving him all alone. He was too lustful a man to endure this for long.

One evening, at dusk, he was out for a walk when he saw a charming girl he had never seen before, and he immediately wanted her. She tried to run away, but he caught her and asked her who she was. Very sweetly she replied, "No one."

Eventually Yoshifuji went with her to the girl's house, a charming house full of servants. That night they slept together. "He was so taken with her that he forgot about his wife, his home and his children; he no longer considered them. He and the girl swore eternal love to each other. His new wife soon became pregnant, and when she gave birth, "Yoshifuji no longer had any interest in the world."

Meanwhile, in his human home, Yoshifuji's disappearance caused a great stir and a thorough search was undertaken, but to no avail. His family prayed, read Buddhist sutras and carved an image of a cannon with eleven heads. The narrative then shifts to Yoshifuji's new home, where a man with a staff immediately appears. Yoshifuji's new family runs away terrified and the man strikes

Yoshifuji, forcing him out through a narrow passageway: "This was the thirteenth night after Yoshifuji disappeared. The people in his old home were still shaking their heads over what had happened, when a strangely dark creature with the appearance of a monkey emerged from the bottom of the warehouse next door. What could it have been? Through the babble of excited onlookers emerged a voice that said, "It's me!" It was Yoshifuji. Yoshifuji told of his wonderful new life and his new son. A servant was sent to investigate the warehouse and the foxes ran off in every direction. There was a small space under the warehouse, "that was where Yoshifuji had been. Obviously a fox had tricked him. He had married a fox and had never returned to sanity." His thirteen days in fox hell seemed like thirteen years to him. A monk and an onmyōji were summoned to pray for him and exorcise him, and he was washed several times.

When he "finally came to his senses he was terribly embarrassed," but he "continued his life in good health for another decade and died in his sixtieth year."

The narrative is extraordinarily complex and presents several perspectives, one man's journey into the underworld of the kitsune kingdom and, simultaneously, the search for his family. The fox itself does not appear as a deceitful demonic monster, but is more like an innocent victim of a man's lecherous desire. Yoshifuji's accidental abandonment of his first wife, followed by the abandonment of his second (fox) wife, suggests that in the gender dynamics of the time, the status of women and foxes may not have been so far apart. As with many setsuwa, the "moral" is not necessarily clear, but at least on a general level we can interpret the narrative as an admonition not to take family for granted. Another famous example where the narrative of fox-man love inspires pathos is the story of Abe no Yasuna, father of the great onmyōji Abe no Seimei. Yasuna is said to have married a white fox named Kuzunoha. The legend appeared at least in early 1662 in a written work called Abe no Seimei monogatari (The Tale of Abe no Seimei) but gained great popularity through its dramatization for puppet theater and Kabuki. The most famous scene in the Kabuki version is the henshin (transformation) in which an actor performs a rapid change from human to fox, a stunt that not only displays the actor's skill and the special effects of Kabuki, but also shows the kitsune's well-known shape-shifting powers.

The stories of kitsune-nyōbo, or fox-wives, were collected in the late 20th century. Yanagita Kunio, for example, documents a tale from a rural area of Ishikawa Prefecture. A man went out one night to go to the bathroom and when he returned inside, he discovered that his wife had duplicated herself. There were now two her's in the room. They were indistinguishable, and the man could not decide which was the real one and which was a bakemono. To do so, he asked them difficult questions to which they both answered with ease. Eventually he decided that one of them was not quite right, so he followed her out and took the other woman as his wife. In the years that followed, the house prospered and the wife gave birth to two children.

One day, the boys were playing hide-and-seek and noticed that their mother had a tail! Now that her true nature had been discovered, the fox wife could no longer stay with the family and left in fear. But during the growing season she appeared again, this time in her fox form, and surrounded the family's rice fields. That year, and in subsequent years, the paddies seemed to be empty, and the tax collector determined that the family had nothing. But when they cut the stalks, brought them into the house and peeled the husks, they found that they were full of rice, and because they did not have to pay taxes on their harvest, the family became rich.

# Chapter 11

The Raccoon Dog

Tanuki are among the most common of all yōkai. Folktales and legends about them are found throughout Japan, and tanukis have long been featured in literature and art, in children's books, and more recently in films, anime, manga, video games, and advertisements. They are usually depicted as supernatural figures, often funny and mischievous, but not necessarily killers although in some narratives they appear as fierce.

Tanukis are real animals: in English they are sometimes called badgers or, more accurately, "raccoon dogs." They are small, mainly nocturnal, omnivorous mammals that look like a cross between a raccoon and a possum. Originally from East Asia, tanuchus have spread to Scandinavia and most of northern Europe.

They have a high reproductive rate, as well as the ability to eat human-prepared food and live near human settlements. The tanuki is a border beast: they ecologically follow the boundary between culture and nature.

The traits of the tanuki animal are reflected in its yōkai image: tanukis seem to exist simultaneously in this world and the other world. In folklore they are tricksters, often portrayed as rather clumsy and pot-bellied, with a penchant for sake, shape-shifters who prefer to impersonate Buddhist monks. One of the tanuki's most famous features is its gigantic scrotum, which it uses for all kinds of creative transformations; numerous woodcuts and other images illustrate the power of this magnificent paraphernalia. Thus, in contemporary Japan, tanukis are a symbol of fertility, a sign of prosperity and good luck: in front of restaurants, bars, and sake stores, one finds ceramic figurines of a tanuki in an upright position, plump, with large eyes, cheerful, and adorned with a straw hat and a sake jug in one hand. On the streets of a modern city, the creature exudes a sense of joviality and traditional welcome.

The first documented appearance of a tanuki-like creature is in the Nihonshoki, where it is called a mujina. During the Heian and Kamakura periods, tanuki began to appear in setsuwa. Uji tales, for example, include the story in which a mountain hermit, after years of deep devotion, begins to receive nightly visits from the Bodhisattva Fugen on his white elephant. One evening a hunter bringing food to the hermit was invited to witness the sacred vision, but when Fugen appeared, emanating a wonderful light, the hunter was suspicious. Why should he, an animal killer, be granted the sight of the divine? So, he put an arrow in his bow and aimed at that figure. The light disappeared and a roar was heard. In the morning, the hunter and the hermit followed a trail of blood to the bottom of a ravine where they found a dead tanuki with an arrow in its chest.

Historically, tanuki are often associated with foxes or kitsune, and in some cases the two creatures are interchangeable; the term kori, combining the idiom of kitsune and tanuki, was used to refer to all kinds of supernatural events. Although generalizations are always difficult to interpret, for the most part kitsune seem to be cunning and dangerous creatures who take the form of an attractive woman; in contrast, tanuki are more fun, often taking the form of a plump monk or other not-so-attractive figures. As in the setsuwa described above, despite the temporary success of their transformation, tanuki always end up being killed.

# Chapter 12

## BANEKO: The Yokai Cat

There are numerous examples of yōkai cats in Japanese culture, in which they are portrayed as anything from carefree tricksters to cruel monsters. Presumably the cat's calm and intelligent appearance, together with its stealthy behavior and powerful vocal abilities, contributes to a sense of mystery and otherworldliness. In Japan, as in many places around the world, cats seem to occupy an ambiguous position in human lives.

They sit quietly, purring, on their laps one minute and then come down to chase a mouse the next. They are both domestic and wild, at home in both urban and rural settings, at once an intimate part of the human world and part of the natural world. Perhaps it is no surprise that cats, both wild and domestic, play an important role in yōkai culture.

A common yōkai cat, the nekomata, is characterized by a forked tail. It was said that when a cat reached a certain age, its tail forked and began to act suspiciously and dangerously. An ancient nekomata story from the year 1233 tells of a creature with eyes like those of a cat and a body like that of a large dog. It devoured seven or eight people in a single night. In many cases nekomata are described as extremely large cats living in mountains and forests, but they can also be found in populous cities and towns.

Toriyama Sekien illustrates a nekomata in his first catalog: it stands on two legs on the outside porch of a house, with a small cloth (tenugui) on its head. Another cat, presumably not a yōkai, sits on the floor below him, while a third appears to be looking out from inside the house. Although Sekien does not explain anything, the nekomata is portrayed somewhere between the world of humans and the natural world. He is wild, but wears a cloth over his head, stands on two legs like a person, and is literally climbing on the outside edge of a human dwelling, with a cat outside, behind, and another inside, in front. The fact that there are no comments suggests that the nekomata was a commonly recognized yōkai that needed no explanation.

Another yōkai cat is called bakeneko, which can be loosely translated as "monster cat." While bakeneko generally appear to be no different from normal cats (they do not have forked tails like a nekomata) their monstrosity is similarly attributed to age. In some parts of Japan, it was said that a domestic cat kept longer than a certain number of years (the exact number varies from place to place) could kill its owner or, more commonly, turn into a bakeneko and perform all kinds of harmful acts. This bad behavior can be comical, speaking with a human voice, for example, or dancing with a cloth on its head, or it can be terrifying such as becoming a person, harassing travelers, possessing people or manipulating the bodies of the dead.

The most famous bakeneko tale is "Nabeshima no bakeneko sōdō" (The Nabeshima bakeneko disturbance), a legend that developed from a succession of disputes, known as the Nabeshima Disturbance, that occurred in Hizen (present-day Saga Prefecture) in the late 1500s. Some versions of the Nabeshima legend are simple revenge tales, while others tell of a plot involving a demonic cat in the guise of a woman that is foiled only by the intense loyalty of one of Nabeshima's family servants. The origin of the narratives themselves probably dates back to the Edo period, long after the original disorder, but they became popular through sensationalist Kabuki and kyōgen plays, as well as through illustrations printed on wooden blocks. In the 20th century, versions of the tale were made into films, such as Hiroku kaibyō-den (The Haunted Castle, 1969, dir. Tanaka Tokuzō).

# Chapter 13

KASA-BAKE The Umbrella Yokai

Although there are no known narratives or folk beliefs associated specifically with the kasa-bake (also called kasa-obake or karakasa-obake), this umbrella monster has become a staple of yōkai iconography, appearing in everything from Edo-period games to contemporary live-action films to anime. The kasa-bake is generally depicted as an old-fashioned Japanese umbrella (made of oiled paper on a bamboo frame) with two arms, an eye, a long tongue, and, instead of a handle, a single leg with a wooden geta sandal. The kasa-bake is a distinctly cheerful and adorable image, especially in the film versions in which it jumps on its one leg.

An umbrella-shaped yōkai appears in an image in an early Edo period scroll, Hyakkiyagyō-zu, attributed to Kanō Tōun (1625-1694). In his

Hyakki tsurezure bukuro of 1784, Toriyama Sekien also includes a yōkai he calls hone-karakasa (bone umbrella). Both of these images, however, are quite different from the one that would become popular in the early years. A particularly representative version of the one-eyed, one-legged, long-tongued kasa-bake is found in an illustrated sugoroku board game (a form of game popular during most of the Edo period) made by Utagawa Yoshikazu. This is the image that, much later, Mizuki Shigeru developed into his manga, and it is also the protagonist used, for example, in the 2005 film The Great Yōkai War.

Whatever its origins, kasa-bake is clearly associated with the concept of tsukumogami, household utensils and objects that become yōkai after a hundred years. Moreover, the nature of the kasa-bake with an eye and a leg suggests that it is cognitively related to many other yōkai, such as hitotsume-kozō, which have an eye or a leg, attributes common to deities and monsters in other cultures as well.

It is equally important to note that, beginning in the Edo period, some umbrellas were known as ja-no-me-gasa, "umbrellas with a snake's eye," but it is unclear whether there is a direct relationship between these and kasa-bake yōkai. Presumably the ja-no-me-gasa were so called because of the colored circle placed around the circumference of the cloth, near the tip. When the umbrella was open, the tip appeared as a single eye of a snake.

# Chapter 14

All Deities from A to Z

阿遅鉏高日子根神: Ajishikitaka Hikone no Kami

Son of Ōkuninushi no Mikoto (大国主命) and Princess Tagori Hime no Mikoto (田心姫命), his sister is Shitateru Hime no Mikoto (下照比売命).

Some people think it is a representation of a grain: it dies in autumn and regenerates in spring. This grain loses its energy in winter and is reborn in the new season. This relationship between agriculture and nature goes back to ancient beliefs, which is why we can represent this god in the form of a snake wandering in the rice fields.

According to the book Izumo no Kuni Fudoki (出雲国風土記), this god cried so much as a child that he had to sail around 80 islands to stop crying. It is said that the god Takitsu Hiko (多伎都比古) accompanied him on the ship during all this time.

Ajishikitaka is worshipped as the god of agriculture, lightning, snakes, and housing. In general, the snake is seen as an animal suitable for agriculture.

When Ame no Waka Hiko (天若日子 - god sent from heaven to pacify Japan) died, the god Ajishikitaka Hikone no Kami descended to Earth to mourn him. He became very angry after being mistaken for the deceased.

Since then, he would remain in the Tarō volcano, around which humans enjoy pure water and beautiful rice fields.

穴穂部間人皇女: Anahobe no Hashihito no Hime Miko

The third daughter of Emperor Kinmei (欽明天皇), she continued the reign of the imperial family during the Asuka period. She would be the biological mother of Shotoku (聖徳太子), the emperor at the origin of the establishment of Buddhism in Japan.

One legend says that her son Shotoku was an envoy of the gods. She would have conceived on her own, by divine will. It is actually more plausible that her father was Emperor Yōmei before he died.

He died in 621, one year before Emperor Shotoku.

## 安閑天皇: Ankan Tennō

Emperor Ankan (466 - January 27, 536) was the 27th emperor of Japan. He reigned from February 7, 531 to December 17, 535.

He succeeded his father, Emperor Keitai (継体天皇), at the age of 66. His reign was very short: he died 4 years later.

His exploits as emperor are narrated in Ankanki (安閑記). He is behind the creation of many Miyakes (屯倉) between Kanto and Kyūshū, that is, areas ruled by the Yamato (Japanese Empire) dedicated to agriculture. This shows the great extent of the Empire at that time.

With the mixture of the gods of Shintoism and Buddhism, Shinbutsu Shūgō (神仏習合), Emperor Ankan merged with the Buddhist deity Zaō Gongen (蔵王権現).

His burial mound is the Takaya Tsukiyama (高屋築山古墳) at 5 Chome Furuichi in Habikino, Osaka Prefecture.

安寧天皇: Annei Tennō

Annei is the third emperor of Japan in Japanese mythology. We do not know whether he actually existed and what he accomplished.

He is one of the emperors affected by the "8 periods without history or legend": Kesshi Hachidai (欠史八代 / 缺史八代). This refers to the period of Japanese history from the 2nd emperor (Suizei - 綏靖天皇) to the 9th emperor (Kaika - 開化天皇), and have no stories about them. Only the Kojiki (古事記) and the Nihon Shoki (日本書紀), the earliest works written in Japan, attest that they are among the deified emperors of Japan.

According to modern historians, these emperors are considered legendary and their existence as historical figures is not proven.

## 武烈天皇: Buretsu Tennō

Buretsu (age 489 - January 9, 507) was the 25th emperor of Japan. He reigned from December 498 to December 8, 506. He is the son of Emperor Ninken (仁賢天皇) and

Princess Kasuga no Ōiratsume no Kōgō (春日大娘皇女).

He is described as a tyrant assassinated by his own people during an uprising. However, this trace is questioned for two reasons:

- The existence of this emperor is questioned.

- It is most likely that the emperor who succeeded him wanted to create a distance between Burestu and himself in order to appear as a better emperor.

The Kojiki (古事記) does not dwell on the emperor's cruelty unlike the Nihon Shoki (日本書紀). His violent, cruel, and sadistic acts describe a character as evil as Emperor Yūryaku (雄略天皇). He is said to have scalped a man and then let him climb a tree. He pulled out every branch until the unfortunate man jumped down. He is also said to have opened the belly of a pregnant woman until the uterus was visible. Other atrocities are cited, one more cruel than the other.

Although the historical texts of Fusō Ryakuki (扶桑略記) tell us that he would have died at the age of 18, this information is not certain. He died without an heir, ending Japan's first dynasty of emperors.

His mausoleum would be the Kanaoka no Iwatsuki no Oka no Kita no Misasagi (傍丘磐坏丘北陵) in Imaizumi, Nara Prefecture.

## 茅渟王: Chinu no Miko

Great-grandson of Emperor Bidatsu (敏達天皇) and son of Ōmata no Miko (大俣王), little information has come down about him. It is known that he gave life to Empress Kōgyoku (皇極天皇) and Kōtoku (孝徳天皇) with his wife Kibi Hime no Ōkimi

(吉備姫王), herself a descendant of Emperor Kinmei (欽明天).

Historian Yoshinobu Tsukaguchi (塚口 義信) lets us think that he would actually be the ruler of the Baekje kingdom in Korea, recorded in the Shinsen Shōjiroku (新撰姓氏録). Chinu's origins on his mother's side remain rather unclear, as if it were an inconvenient truth. Ancient writings do not allow us to truly understand Chinu's origin, and thus the origin of his descendants.

Nothing is known about his achievements during his lifetime.

仲哀天皇: Chūai Tennō

Emperor Chūai (148 - March 8, 200), is the 14th Japanese emperor. His reign lasted from February 11, 192 to March 8, 200.

He succeeded his uncle Emperor Seimu (成務天皇), who had no successor. As the son of Yamato Takeru (日本武尊), unifier of Japan at the time, his power is legitimate.

Legend says that the gods told the emperor that wealth was waiting for him across the sea and that he would return triumphant. The emperor doubted the truth of these words and preferred to do nothing. His actions went against his father's philosophy of conquest. Chūai went to fight the rebellious Kumaso (熊襲) people of Kyūshū and lost his life.

His wife, Empress Jingū (神功皇后), avenged the emperor and subdued the Kumaso. He is said to have conquered Korea at that time after his death. The gods had warned Chūai that the fate that had been proposed to him would then rightfully belong to his son, Ōjin Tennō (応神天皇). The land returned to Ōjin after Empress Jingū's great conquest.

恵美須大神: Ebisu Ōkami

God of prosperity in business, Ebisu is one of the seven gods of fortune. He is usually seen in a hunting outfit, holding a fishing rod in his right hand and a sea bream in his left.

The word "Ebisu" also refers to Daidogei (a street performance in which performers use a doll) with an Ebisu dancing as a blessing for the beginning of spring. This dance is called Ebisu Mawashi (恵比須回し).

His origin is often considered foreign in Japan, sometimes giving him the status of a pagan god. For this reason, many temples dedicated to him accommodate other deities.

His first literary appearance seems to date back to the 12th century, in the Iroha Jiruishō (色葉字類抄), a dictionary listing the characters of Buddhist chants called Iroha (いろは).

He is also likened to Hiruko no Mikoto (蛭子神) from the Muromachi period, a god who was abandoned because he could not stand on his legs after he turned 3 years old. This malformed child (without bones or arms or legs) came from the Izanami - Izanagi couple after Izanami wanted to marry Izanagi. They threw him back into the sea, unable to accept his situation. It is said that his malformation is due to the fact that only the male god can propose marriage. If it is the woman who proposes, then the couple will be unhappy.

It is also symbolized by the whale (called Kujira - クジラ or Isa - 勇魚) as it indicates abundant fishing for fishermen. In fact, he who says whale says fish. It is said that after being thrown back into the sea , it would be able to form legs even though its body is not perfect. It is sometimes attributed to jellyfish, capable of moving without bones. Jellyfish are recurrent in the motifs of his clothing.

Ebisu is a deity found in many harbors and fishing villages in Japan. In the past, a beached whale was a sign of Ebisu to fight famine.

Cults linking Ebisu and the sea are quite common: it is said that collecting debris from the sea from abroad will be rewarded by Ebisu, that any living remnant brought from the sea is called "Ebisu," or that stones in the sea can be objects of worship to pray to Ebisu.

Ancestral customs tell us something interesting to understand this god. As a sea god, he can be differentiated from a mountain god: for people inland, the spirits of the deceased go up the rivers to find peace in the mountains, while for people on the coast, the deceased must join the gods in eternity across the sea. This is why, among other things, it is said that Ebisu can appear and come from the sea.

Many businesses come to pray at temples connected to Ebisu to bring them luck and prosperity in trade. This custom originated in the late Heian period when Ebisu became a deity of the city markets. One thing led to another, Ebisu became a deity of trade and took on the face attributed to him today: smiling and chubby.

Anyone who worships him must keep in mind that Ebisu is hard of hearing, even deaf! That is why it is customary to make noise before dedicating prayers to him.

## 太玉命: Futodama no Mikoto

With Ame no Koyane no Mikoto (天児屋命), he offered the legendary mirror Yata no Kagami (八咫鏡) to the goddess Amaterasu (天照) as he left the Amano-Iwato cave (天岩戸). He is a god related to divination rituals, which he performed in the legendary cave. Futodama no Mikoto decorated 500 Japanese trees (sakaki) with mirrors and magatami in remembrance of this moment.

During the Tenson Kōrin (天孫降臨), he descended to Earth with Ninigi no Mikoto (邇邇芸命). He is also the divine guardian of the Ise Shrine. He is considered the ancestor of the Inbe clan (伊部氏).

## 源正霊神: Genshō Reijin

Gensho Reijin is the divine name of the heroic Kamakura samurai Gongorō Kagemasa

(鎌倉権五郎). This late Heian period warlord served in the army during the Gosannen War (奥州後三年記: 1083 - 1087). He was only 16 years old, but he fought with vigor and determination, even though he lost an eye during a battle.

This war scene is depicted in Kabuki theater through the opera Shibaraku (暫).

He is the first to take the name Kamakura, coming from the residence of his father who was a high official of the Taira clan. The city of Kamakura will actually take this name under Minamoto no Yoritomo (源頼朝) in 1085 when he founded the first shogunate: the Kamakura bakufu (鎌倉幕府).

波比岐神: Hahiki no Kami

He is one of the 5 deities known under the generic name of Ikasuri no Mikannagi no Matsuru Kami (坐摩巫祭神), organized by the

Department of Shintō Affairs (Jingi-kan - 神祇官) in the 7th century AD. The 5 gods are:

- Ikuwi no Kami (生井神): protector of life

- Sakuwi no Kami (福井神): a lucky person

- Tsunagawi no Kami (綱長井神): brings good luck when fishing

- Hahiki no Kami (波比祇神): protector of the home and garden

- Asuha no Kami (阿須波神): protector of walkers and travelers

He is the guardian deity of the place of residence, the one who protects the fertile land and whom we pray to have a lush garden. He represents the foundation of a residential site.

Note: Previously, Japanese writing included multiple characters including ゐ: wi. This is why these gods are written with a "wi" that has now disappeared.

## 火遠理命: Hōri no Mikoto

Son of Kono Hana no Sakuya (木花佐久夜毘売命) and Ninigi no Mikoto (邇邇芸命), he is one of the fire-born siblings.

Legend says that Kono Hana no Sakuya became pregnant with Ninigi. This became mad with joy! But very quickly, Kono Hana's belly became bigger and bigger. It was so fast that Ninigi doubted her, thinking it was someone else's child.

Offended, Kono Hana said, "If it is your child, then it will come out of childbirth alive. If not, he will burn in the house where I offer him life." At the moment of birth, Kono Hana set fire to the house to prove her words. In fact, there were three deities that came out of her womb:

- Hoderi no Mikoto (火照命): represents the burning flame, appearing when the fire is at its strongest. Hoderi is the fisherman, a maritime hunter at heart, the one who handles the hook much better than anyone else.

- Hosuseri no Mikoto (火須勢理命): is the flame that persists, born in the midst of fire.

- Hōri no Mikoto (火遠理命): represents the flickering flame. He was born when the fire was about to die. Hōri is the earthly hunter, the one who wields the bow and arrow like no other.

Hōri can be found in the story "Yamasachi Hiko to Umisachi Hiko" (山幸彦と海幸彦 - The gods of the sea and fortune in the mountains) of the Kojiki (古事記), as the mountain god (山幸彦). The god of the sea is Hoderi (海幸彦).

The story begins with a crazy idea that comes from the spirit of Hōri and Hoderi, which is to exchange their tools to break the routine. The hunter becomes a fisherman and vice versa. Hoderi learns to handle the bow and Hōri tries to use the hook so dear to his brother.

Hōri inadvertently drops the hook into the water and is unable to get his hands back on it. Hōri learns the news just as they were to return their sacred instruments. Saddened in his heart, he decides never to speak to his brother again.

Hōri was hurt by this decision. He returned to the water to search for the hook again and again, but to no avail.

The god Shiotsuchi no Kami (塩椎神) approached him through the waves and saw a god full of despair. He listened to him tell his story and then convinced him to join the kingdom of the sea god Ōwatatsumi no Kami (大綿積神) to find a solution. Hōri then boarded a boat, propelled by the tides and ocean currents.

There he met Toyo-tama (豊玉), daughter of King Ōwatatsumi. Hōri fell in love and they were united. The king, in the form of a dragon, asked all the fish to find the lost hook. One bream returned with the famous tool stuck in its cheek.

Ōwatatsumi detached it and returned it to Hōri with an important instruction :

"You must return this hook with your back turned, uttering the spell that impoverishes and makes weak in spirit. If your brother cultivates his field on high, you must plow yours in the valley. You will not tell him until three years from now, after which he will be ruined. If at that time he sends his troops to attack you, then you will drown his soldiers with the sacred stone that raises the water level (Shiomitsu no Tama - 潮満珠).

When he surrenders, he saves his army by using Shiohiru no Tama (潮干珠), the precious stone that brings down the water level."

Ōwatatsumi then summoned crocodiles and sharks to escort Hōri.

Because Hoderi had lost his fetish hook, his fishing was disastrous. The reunion with his hook transformed his fishing and his character. But he was ruined in just under three years after his brother's return. In desperation, he sent his army to sack Hōri's castle.

To defend himself, Hōri used the first gem: the waters suddenly rose and Hoderi and his army nearly drowned. At the last moment, the youngest son used the second gem. The older brother resigned and promised to always be there to protect him.

When he returned to Hōri, his girlfriend gave birth to a child on a beach but refused to let her lover go into labor. So, as he had promised, he came to witness the birth. He was horrified to see his wife's true form, a sea creature somewhere between a fish and a crocodile. Saddened and angry, she fled, abandoning her baby. The orphan was abandoned in a hut made of cormorant feathers. His name was Ugayafukiaezu no Mikoto (鸕鷀草葺不合尊), himself an ancestor of Japan's imperial lineage.

## 伊斯許理度売命: Ishikori Dome no Mikoto

Ishikori Dome is the god of mirrors. He is the one who created the Yata no Kagami, a legendary mirror that reflected the rays of Amaterasu (天照) when the sun goddess was hiding in the Amano-Iwato cave (天岩戸).

The Ishikori Dome is revered by mirror makers and stonemasons.

He is one of the 5 Itsutomono Ono Kami (五伴緒神) who descended to Earth with Nigihayahi no Mikoto (饒速日命).

### 伊奢沙別命: Izasawake no Mikoto

Izasawake is the god of food. He is recognized as the one who is able to perform miracles concerning food. That is why his name is sometimes spelled with the kanji 笥飯, reminiscent of Japan's sacred food: rice. A symbol of peaceful life on Earth, it represents harmonious existence, that which does not go hungry.

It protects those who engage in navigation and enables the prosperity of sea fishing.

Izasawake no Mikoto also oversees industrial development.

### 神世七代: Kami no Yonanayo.

It is a term that includes the 7 gods that come after the Kotoamatsukami deities (別天津神), who appeared at the creation of the Earth.

In addition to the first 2 of the Kami no Yonanayo, who are born and then hidden, the others are sexed. There is a male and a female version:

- Kuni no Tokotachi no Kami (国之常立神)

- Toyogumonu no Kami (豊雲野神)

- Uhijini no Kami (宇比地邇神 - ♂) and Sujijini no Kami (須比智邇神 - ♀)

- Tsunugui no Kami (角杙神 - ♂) and Ikugui no Kami (活杙神 - ♀)

- Ooto no Ji no Kami (意富斗能地神 - ♂) and Ooto no Be no Kami (大斗乃弁神 - ♀)

- Omodaru no Kami (淤母陀琉神 - ♂) and Ayakashikone no Kami (阿夜訶志古泥神 - ♀)

- Izanagi no Kami (伊邪那岐神 - ♂) and Izanami no Kami (伊邪那美神 - ♀)

金山彦神: Kanayama Hiko no Kami

During the creation of the gods, the goddess Izanami suffered burns to her genitals after the birth of Kagutsuchi (軻遇突智), god of fire. Then Izanami suffered a serious illness that caused her to vomit, from which Kanayama Hiko and Kanayama Hime were born.

The word Kanayama (金山) means "gold mine," which is why all mines have these two deities as their god. In addition, they are the protectors of mining, metallurgy, and metallurgists. Metals are mythologically associated with Izanami's vomit, as matter escapes from his mouth.

吉備津彦命: Kibitsu Hiko no Mikoto

Kibitsu was the third prince of Emperor Kōrei (孝霊天皇) and Princess Yamato no Kunika Hime (倭国香媛). He is the half-brother of Wakatake Hiko no Mikoto (雅武彦命).

He would form the Shidō shōgun (四道将軍) with 3 other commanders sent by Emperor Sujin to pacify various regions:

- Ōbiko no Mikoto was sent to the North (Hokurikudō)

- Takenunakawake no Mikoto to the East (Tokaidō)

- Kibitsuhiko no Mikoto in the West (San'yōdō)

- Tanba no Michi no Ushi no Mikoto in the South (Tanba province).

Legend says he defeated the demon Ura (温羅) who was terrorizing Kibi Province (吉備国) from Ki Castle (鬼ノ城). This castle still exists in Sōja, in present-day Okayama Prefecture. Kibitsu is said to have sealed the demon's head under a cauldron in the Kibitsu Shrine (吉備津神社). It is said that the demon's body was given to dogs to graze and its head kept growling under the temple.

During ancient Japan, this practice was quite common. The cauldron had the same value as the terracotta figures called Haniwa (埴輪). The noise emanating from the cauldron (odoji) was a sign of good or bad omen. The connection between this sacred cauldron and this type of ritual is all the stronger because this practice originated in Kibi province.

Together with his half-brother, they are the ones who inspired the folk tale of Momotarō (桃太郎), this young boy seeking riches in the land of demons.

孝昭天皇: Kōshō Tennō

He was the fifth emperor of Japan in Japanese mythology. We do not know whether he actually existed and what he accomplished.

He is one of the emperors affected by the "8 periods without history or legend": Kesshi Hachidai (欠史八代 / 缺史八代). This refers to the period of Japanese history from the 2nd emperor, Suizei (綏靖天皇) to the 9th emperor, Kaika (開化天皇), and has no stories about them. Only the Kojiki (古事記) and the Nihon Shoki (日本書紀), the earliest works written in Japan, attest that they are among the deified emperors of Japan.

According to modern historians, these emperors are considered legendary and their existence as historical figures is not proven.

熊野忍隅命: Kumanōshikuma no Mikoto

He is one of the 5 of the males born from the oath of trust between Amaterasu (天照) and his brother Susanoo (素戔嗚命). He is sometimes referred to as Kumanokusubi (クマノクスビ) because he is a mysterious divine spirit symbolized by a strange fire.

Kumanōshikuma no Mikoto is said to have been born from the jewels of Amaterasu's (天照) hairstyle, crushed by Susanoo (素戔嗚命 ), when the divine sulfur and the mist it emanated met.

明治天皇: Meiji Tennō

Emperor Meiji (November 3, 1852 - July 30, 1912) was the 122nd emperor of Japan. His reign lasted from February 3, 1867 until his death on July 30, 1912.

He is known for changing Japan from the feudal era to modernity, using European powers as a model. He abolished the shogunates, opened the country to foreign trade and increased military power to expand beyond its borders.

The reforms carried out by the emperor went against what Japan had known until now. The military could no longer be involved in power, the samurai could no longer exercise, the shogun era was over, and the first Constitution of the Japanese Empire (大日本帝国憲法) was written in 1889.

With the introduction of a constitutional monarchy, the emperor developed education (with a predilection for teaching Confucius) and sought to unite his people under a common identity.

He is the origin of the Tokyo Imperial Palace (Kōkyo - 皇居), the name change from Edo to Tokyo, and the concept of "1 emperor for 1 era" (Issei Ichi Gen so sei - 一世一元の制).

In addition to these enlightened measures, the emperor maintained conservative beliefs.

Shinto became the state religion (Kokka Shintō 国家神道 国家神道) to unite his people on the one hand and to strengthen the legitimacy of power with religion on the other.

The legendary warrior Kusu no Ki Masashige (楠木正成) became, in addition to being among the deities of Shintoism, a symbol of loyalty to Japanese imperialism.

For his involvement in the Anglo-Japanese military alliance and the Russo-Japanese War, he was decorated with the Order of the Garter in 1906 by England.

As for his personality, he was known to be an emperor with a great memory and able to satisfy himself with what little he had. He was not looking for "the most beautiful castle" or the most flamboyant dress. He loved poetry, riding horses or playing Kemari (蹴鞠 - ancient Chinese military sport, similar to soccer). The emperor called his wife and the ladies of his court by the nicknames he invented, just for fun.

He now rests at Fushimi no Momoyama no Misasagi (伏見桃山陵) in Kyoto.

In 1920, the great shrine Meiji-jingū (明治神宮) was dedicated to the memory of his wife Empress Shōken (昭憲皇后) and her, on the grounds of Yoyogi Park in Tokyo. Yoyogi was the former training ground of the Imperial Japanese Army.

:宮簀媛命 Miyazu Hime no Mikoto

Miyazu Hime is the wife of Yamato Takeru. The legendary sword Kusanagi no Tsurugi (草薙の剣) was offered by the goddess Amaterasu (天照) to her husband to conquer Japan as a descendant of the gods.

As he passed by the river a beautiful girl who was washing his clothes asked her for directions. She made him think she was deaf so she would not answer him. Later, after his expedition eastward, Yamato Takeru went to Owari because the gods had assured him that he would find a wife there. She was Miyazu Hime: the young woman by the river.

They married and, it is said, consummated the marriage through a moon veil.

He is said to have left her the sword after learning that there was an angry deity on Mount Ibuki (伊吹山) in the ancient province of Ōmi (近江国 - present-day Shiga Prefecture). He wanted to get rid of it with his bare hands, and when he arrived at the site, a god blocked his way. Thinking it was not what he was looking for, he turned into a huge snake (or a giant white boar, depending on the version). He threw ice on Yamato Takeru, who lost his way in the mountain until he fainted. He managed to find his way down the mountain, weak, and arrived near a water source. Fate befell him: he became seriously ill as a result of this misadventure. Wanting to go to Ise, he made a detour to Owari to find his companion and his sword. His strength was running out. He died after writing to his wife to watch over his sword.

That is why Miyazu Hime built the Atsuta Shrine-jingū (熱田神宮) to protect her late husband's sword.

The lunar veil, mentioned above during the union of Miyazu Hime and Yamato Takeru is also known as the "lunar obstacle." It must be seen here as a sterile sexual act, which cannot give life. Clearly, Miyazu Hime was indisposed to make love, but the act took place anyway . We can see here Yamato Takeru's affront to nature, all the pride of being proud enough to fight a god with his bare hands or to ignore a deity who confronts him. These 3 elements together could have caused Yamato Takeru to lose the support of the gods and his life.

She is the daughter of Owari no Kuni no Miyatsuko (尾張国造), of the Owari clan (尾張氏), and the younger sister of Take Inadane no Mikoto (建稲種命). Miyazu Hime is known as the priestess of the Owari clan.

仁徳天皇: Nintoku Tennō

Nintoku is the 16th emperor of Japan. According to official texts, he was born in 290 and reigned from 313 to 399. He is the fourth son of Emperor Ōjin (応神天皇).

Upon Ōjin's death, Uji no Wakiiratsuko (菟道稚郎子) was to ascend the throne. He was Ōjin's most influential son. He preferred to commit suicide and leave his place to his brother who later became Emperor Nintoku. A period of three years elapsed before the throne was occupied.

A folk writing (民のかまど) tells us that he was listening to his people. One day, when he noticed that no smoke was coming out of a poor man's house, he decided to stop demanding taxes for 3 years from all his people. The quality of life of every resident improved. Once the taxes were returned, he used the fortune to carry out large-scale irrigation projects and to acquire large tracts of land. Because of these achievements he was called Hijiri no Mikado (聖帝), that is, the Holy Emperor.

Although he is shown as a great humanist, every man has his flaws.

Some sources indicate that Emperor Nintoku loved female beauty to the point of driving his wife, Empress Iwa no hime (磐姫皇后), crazy with jealousy. He would be attracted to other women such as the resplendent Kuro Hime (黒日売) or a maid named Kuwata no Kuga Hime (桑田玖賀媛). The former was too afraid of the empress to attempt a fling with the emperor, and the latter was chased out of the palace by Iwa no Hime.

It is possible that she accepted even less Yata no Hime Miko because she was a high-ranking princess, daughter of Emperor Ōjin (応神天皇 - the 15th emperor of Japan).

Emperor Nintoku's mausoleum is the Kofun Daisenryō (大仙陵古墳) in Sakai, Osaka Prefecture.

## 織田 信長: Oda Nobunaga

Oda Nobunaga (June 23, 1534 - June 21, 1582) was a warlord and feudal lord from the Sengoku period (戦国時) to the Azuchi Momoyama period (安土桃山时代). He was the first of Japan's three great heroes.

The 3 unifiers of Japan appear in this chronological order:

- Oda Nobunaga (織田信長)

- Toyotomi Hideyoshi (豊臣秀吉)

- Tokugawa Ieyasu (徳川家康)

The son of a modest lord, he becomes an unparalleled conqueror. Although he has a rather atypical behavior that earned him the nickname "High Idiot" (大うつけ - Ō utsusuke) during his youth, his military exploits are numerous. He destroyed a plethora of clans to extend his power and to break any possible resistance.

Oda Nobunaga revolutionized warfare by favoring new combat techniques (firearms, large spears, reinforced ships,...) and developed the local economy to improve the national economy. He opened Japan to foreign trade (China, Korea, the Netherlands, Portugal, ...) and laid the foundation for an international policy that Ieyasu Tokugawa would later develop.

Although he was a man of incomparable violence, he developed Japanese art to glorify his reign. The most beautiful castle in Japan, the Azuchi-jō (安土城), became proof of his brilliant power. Culture was not in order because it was under Oda Nobunaga that Sen no Rikyū (千利休) established the tea ceremony.

He ended his life by becoming Seppuku (切腹) during the Honnō-ji Incident (本能寺の変). The samurai Akechi Mitsuhide (明智光秀) rebels against Nobunaga and forces him to commit suicide after defeating his army. This episode remains of historical concern because the remains of Oda Nobunaga have not been found. It is possible that it was actually a coup organized by Tokugawa Ieyasu (徳川家康).

Its achievements are celebrated every year during the Kiyosu-jō Nobunaga Matsuri (清洲城信長まつり).

On the day of the event, the entire Kiyosu Castle area is the scene of countless attractions and activities organized by the city of Kiyosu (fireworks demonstrations, samurai parade, performances, ...).

大国主命: Ōkuninushi no Mikoto

A direct descendant of Susanoo (素戔嗚命), Ōkuninushi is the one who unites and dominates the vast territories.

Sources in Shintoism indicate various origins in relation to Susanoo (素戔嗚命):

According to the text of the Nihon Shoki (日本書紀), Ōkuninushi no Mikoto is described as the son of Susanoo's son, while the Kojiki (古事記) depicts him as the great-grandson of the sixth generation descended from Susanoo.

He is also said to be the god of tolerance, agriculture, medicine and business. His influence in Shinto mythology is important.

Ōkuninushi worked on the creation of Ashihara no Nakatsukuni 原中国, the land between Heaven and Hell. It is actually a metaphor for Japan, a wet land where reeds (Ashi) grow.

Although he was rightfully on the throne of the god Susanoo (素戔嗚命), he left it to the thunder god Takemikazuchi no Mikoto (武甕槌命). Then he allied with Ninigi no Mikoto (邇邇芸命), a direct descendant of Amaterasu (天照). Ninigi ruled the visible world while Ōkuninushi became the lord of the invisible world (Tokoyo - 常世).

The souls of the deceased go to Ōkuninushi's spiritual realm, Tokoyo, while the bodies go to the Yomi (黄泉).

When it was necessary to support Ōkuniushi to complete the construction of the earth, the Sukuna god Hiko Na no Mikoto (少彦名命) invented remedies for ailments. He also brought ritual spells for protection. Thanks to Sukuna Hiko and from the story of the white rabbit, Ōkuninushi is said to protect against disease and heal animals.

The legend of the white rabbit (因幡の白兎, Inaba no Shirousagi) tells that his 80 brothers (the Yasogami - 八十) are said to have encountered a dying white rabbit on a beach. The rabbit, whose fur had been torn off by crocodiles, begged for help. The mischievous gods advised him to rinse himself in the salt water of the sea and then go to rest on top of a mountain where the wind blows hard. The rabbit's suffering worsened and the gods laughed at his misfortune.

Ōkuninushi saw the poor rabbit, alone and sobbing. The rabbit explained everything to the gods, from his misadventure with crocodiles to the wickedness of the gods. Ōkuninushi felt as much pity for the animal as he did for his brothers. He advised him to take therapeutic remedies, including pure water from a spring not far from the rabbit and plants that would calm him. Thanks to

Ōkuninushi, the rabbit regained his white fur. He took revenge on the 80 gods and became the matchmaker between Yagami Hime - 八上比売 (coveted by the 80 gods) and his savior.

Furious, the 80 brothers decided to kill Ōkuninushi. From a mountaintop, they sent him a fiery rock in the shape of a boar. Thinking it was a deity, he tried to stop it and burned to death. His mother, Sashikuni Waka Hime (刺国若比売), invoked Kamimusuhi (神産巣日神) to bring him back to life. But his brothers killed him a second time, crushing him between two parts of a tree that closed in on him. Sashikuni Waka Hime again asked Kamimusuhi to bring him back to life, and he did.

To avoid dying again, Ōkuninushi decided to go to Susanoo (素戔嗚命) in the Underworld for advice.

After Ōkuninushi lost his land during the Tenson Kōrin (天孫降臨) and went down to the Underworld, Takamimusuhi no Kami (高御産巣日神) came back to him and said:

"If you say you want to take an earthly deity as your wife (Kunitsukami - 国津神), then your heart has not yet forgiven the deities of heaven (Amatsukami - 天津神). Take my daughter, Mihotsu Hime (三穂津姫命), as your wife, and lead the 80,000 gods together to protect the eternal imperial lineage."

Ōkuninushi accepted and regained a place worthy of the greatest deities of Shintō.

Since then, he welcomes the gods to Izumo Shrine once a year for the Kannazuki (神無月 - annual meeting of the gods), during the 10th lunar month .

One story says that an earth god (土地の神) was furiously jealous when he heard that

Nunakawa Hime no Mikoto (沼河比売) would marry Ōkuninushi. They faced each other in a speed race. The earth god rode a black horse with blue hair and Ōkuninushi used an ox. They had to ride one of the mountains of Besshō (別所) to decide who deserved the beautiful goddess more (although in reality the goddess would not go back on her decision).

The horse arrived at the top of the mountain and left its mark by scratching a rock. At the same time, the ox had also reached the top but on the other side! It also left its mark by scratching a rock.

Going into a black rage, the earth god demanded revenge from Ōkuninushi. He agreed, but the earth god's fury blinded him so much that he let his horse escape into the sky. The horse then fell back onto the rocky mountain in the shape of the animal.

It is because of this story that we can still find the trace of the ox or the horse on the rocky mountain today.

大鳥連祖神: Ōtori no Murajin Oyagami

Main deity of the Ōtori-taisha shrine (大鳥神社) in Sakai city, he is said to have originated from Izumi province (currently grouped into the Osaka region).

Since his ancestor was the god Ame no Koyane no Mikoto (天児屋根命), he is likened to it.

He shares the Ōtori shrine (大鳥大社) with Yamato Takeru (日本武尊) after Yamato Takeru turned into a swan there to reach Amaterasu (天照) in the sky. That is why the two characters intermingle and why this temple was once a place of veneration for the goddess Amaterasu (天照).

The Ōtori clan (大鳥氏) claimed to be a descendant of this god and thus of the god Ame no Koyane no Mikoto.

## 履中天皇: Richū Tennō

Richū was the 17th emperor of Japan, son of Nintoku (仁徳天皇) and Iwa no Hime no Mikoto (磐之媛命).

He is known for establishing a National History system with secretaries of state (Fumihito - 国史) to mark the identity of the Japanese people. He led a more comprehensive national policy, including a Ministry of War (Kura no Tsukasa - 蔵職). Later, his influence declined: by attempting to tax Tsukushi Province (筑紫国 - in present-day Fukuoka Prefecture), he was cursed by the gods and lost the empress.

He died 6 years after coming to power. His age varies according to sources: 70 years according to the Nihon Shoki (日本書紀), 64 years in the Kojiki (古事記) and 67 years according to the Jinnō shōtōki (神皇正統記). He lies in the Kamiishizu Misanzai mausoleum (百舌鳥耳原南陵) in Sakai, Osaka Prefecture.

嵯峨天皇: Saga Tennō

Emperor Saga (October 3, 786 - August 24, 842) was the 52nd emperor of Japan. He reigned from May 18, 809 to May 29, 823. According to the historical corpus Rikkokushi (六国史), he changed his name from Kamino to Saga after his death.

It is said that he was intelligent, liked to read, had the charisma of a ruler, and was loved by his father Emperor Kanmu (桓武天皇).

He is also said to have been the first to integrate tea into Japanese culture. It was in 815 that he took tea prepared by the monk Eichū (永忠) of the Tang Dynasty (唐朝).

He made the decision to abolish the death penalty in 818 and banned the sacrifice of animals (except fish) in temples. This was mainly due to the Buddhist influence of the time, which regarded all life as sacred. The death penalty did not reappear until 338 years later.

One of the "3 brushes (三筆)" of the Heian period, he is a renowned calligrapher and a wise connoisseur of the things of this world. He is particularly interested in Chinese poetry and calligraphy. He is best known for his calligraphic works such as the Kōjōki Kaichou (光定戒牒) of the Enryaku-ji Buddhist Monastery (延暦寺) and for being the originator of the Saga Go-ryū (嵯峨御流) school of flower arrangement (Ikebana).

In a collection of stories, the Nihon Ryōiki (日本国現報善悪霊異記), it is said that a monk from Mount Ishizuchi (石鎚山) in Iyo Province

(伊豫国) was reincarnated as emperor after his death. His name was Jousen (寂仙). The Buddhist monk is believed to have reincarnated as Emperor Saga after saying at his death (758), "I will return in 28 years as the emperor's son and my name will be Kamino." The emperor had a son exactly 28 years later, the locals remembered this prophecy and saw in him the Buddhist monk of old.

His mausoleum is the Saga no Yama no E no Misasagi (嵯峨山上), in Kyoto.

齊明天皇: Saimei Tennō

Empress Saimei ruled Japan twice, under 2 names. She was the first woman to enter the Japanese throne:

- As Empress Saimei (斉明天皇): from January 15, 642 to June 14, 645, as the 35th imperial ruler.

- As Empress Kōgyoku (皇極天皇): from January 3, 655 to July 24, 661, as the 37th imperial ruler.

The Isshi Incident (乙巳の変) of 645, in which a conspiracy to produce in front of the Empress and against the main branch of the Soga clan, led Empress Saimei to abdicate. She was replaced by Emperor Kōtoku (孝徳天皇), before becoming empress again 10 years later. Although the tragic event took place in Itabuki Palace (板蓋宮), she resumed her duties there.

His mausoleum is the burial mound of Kurumaki Kennou Kofun (車木ケンノウ古墳) in Takatori-cho, Takaichi-gun, Nara Prefecture. Other sources indicate that he is said to rest in Asuka, either in the Kengoshizuka Kofun burial mound (牽牛子塚古墳) or the Iwayama Kofun burial mound (岩屋山古墳). It is also possible that it is in the Kotani Kofun mound (小谷古墳) in Kashihara.

寒川比古命: Samukawa Hiko no Mikoto

Samukawa Hiko no Mikoto (寒川比古命) and Samukawa Hime no Mikoto (寒川比女命) are the pioneers of the Kanto region. Together they are also called "Samukawa Daimyojin" (寒川大明神).

They are the Guardian Spirits (守護神 守護神) of the "Eight Directions" (八方除), i.e., of all directions, who protect against all misfortunes that may occur (family, natural disasters, business, etc.).

Samukawa Shrine (寒川神社) has been worshipped by Japanese people all over the country for 1,600 years.

寒川比女命: Samukawa Hime no Mikoto

Samukawa Hiko no Mikoto (寒川比古命) and Samukawa Hime no Mikoto (寒川比女命) are the pioneers of the Kanto region. Together they are also called "Samukawa Daimyojin" (寒川大明神).

They are the Guardian Spirits (守護神 守護神) of the "Eight Directions" (八方除), i.e., of all directions, who protect against all misfortunes that may occur (family, natural disasters, business, etc.).

Samukawa Shrine (寒川神社) has been worshipped by Japanese people all over the country for 1,600 years.

成務天皇: Seimu Tennō

Emperor Seimu (84 - July 30, 190) was the 13th emperor of Japan. He reigned from February 19, 131 to July 30, 190.

His father was Emperor Keikō (景行天皇) and his mother was Yasakairi Hime (八坂入媛命).

He established the national government in the large and small provinces, small and large prefectures, and the Sakai region. For this he needed the help of Take no uchi no Sukune (武内宿禰), whom he appointed Grand Minister (大臣). He organized the country so that people could live in peace, particularly by creating borders following rivers and mountains and installing power representatives in each prefecture and county. These representatives are called Kunizukuri (国郡) and Inagi (県邑).

His mausoleum is the Sasaishizuka Yama Kofun (佐紀石塚山古) in Nara Prefecture.

Although this information has come down to us through the Nihon Shoki (日本書紀), there is still doubt about the existence of this emperor. Various historical elements remain unclear or even distorted.

## 清寧天皇: Seinei Tennō

Emperor Seinei (444 - February 27, 484) was the 22nd emperor of Japan. He reigned from January 15, 480 to January 16, 484.

3rd prince of Emperor Yūryaku (雄略天皇), his mother would be Katsuragi no Kara Hime (葛城韓媛) His father would choose him by intuition thinking he would be a worthy successor.

He was called Shiraga (白髪 - white hair) because he had white hair from birth.

He rose to power after the rebellion of Prince Hoshikawa (星川皇子の乱), his brother who tried to usurp power. The prince was burned in the building where he had taken refuge, along with most of those who accompanied him.

His greatest concern was that he had no successor. He decided to bring to the palace the brothers Woke and Oke, sons of Prince Ichinohe no Oshiwa no Miko (市辺押磐皇子) who was killed by Emperor Yūryaku. Both later became emperors.

He is said to rest in the Shiragayama Kofun (浦白髪山古墳) in Habikino (Osaka).

## 昭憲皇太后: Shōken Kōtaigō

Shōken Kōtaigō (昭憲皇太后) was born in 1849 and was the third daughter of leftist Prime Minister Ichijo Tadaka (一条 忠香). At that time his name was Masako Ichijō (一条勝子).

On December 26, 1869, she changed her first name to Haruko (美) and was promoted to Jusanmi (正三位). This religious rank placed her on the divine level of a ruler. Then she married Emperor Meiji (明治天皇) with whom she reigned over Japan as empress. She gave a boost to a Japan in the midst of modernization following the overthrow of the Tokugawa shogunate. Power finally passed from a feudal lord to a legitimate emperor.

She is the first woman emperor to be involved in public life and politics. She participated in the visits of heads of state / presidents / kings / princes ... for diplomatic purposes. Empress Haruko became her husband's true right-hand man when he was unable to rule, both in the affairs of the imperial court and in leading the army.

Her philanthropy led her to create the Japanese Red Cross of the time: the Imperial Shouken Koutai Goukikin Fund (昭憲皇太后基金). Haruko is also involved in the development of women's education with the O-cha no Mizu Normal School in Tokyo.

She is said to be a prodigy from childhood and is loved by her people. This modern empress adapts to her time, even going so far as to exchange her traditional dress for European clothes. She is also the first empress to show herself in such clothes, as early as 1886.

Haruko became Empress Dowager (Kōtaigō) in 1912, upon the death of her husband. She is thus the regent of the future Emperor Taishō (大正天皇).

She died in 1914, taking the posthumous title of Shōken Kōtaigō. His tomb is at the Fushimi no Momo Yama no Misasagi (伏見桃山東陵) in Kyoto and is venerated at the Meiji Jingu Shrine in Tokyo.

## 垂仁天皇: Suinin Tennō

Suinin is the 11th emperor of Japan (January 27, 69 BC - August 8, 70 BC). He reigned from July 14, 99 BC to August 8, 70 BC. Although there is no actual evidence of his existence, it is traditionally accepted by the Japanese people.

It was under his reign that the Great Shrine of Ise was built. According to legend in the Nihon Shoki (日本書紀), the emperor ordered his daughter Yamato Hime no Mikoto (倭比売命) to find a permanent place to worship the goddess Amaterasu (天照). After 20 years searching for the best place, she had the inner shrine of Ise (Naiku) built at the request of the goddess and after being guided by Izawatomi no Mikoto (伊佐波登美命). It was during the reign of Emperor Suinin that the first High Priestess (Saiō) was appointed to the Great Shrine of Ise.

However, other sources indicate that the first Saiō to serve at Ise was Princess Ōku, under Emperor Tenmu (天武天皇).

It is also under Suinin that the first worship of the deity Kono Hana Sakuya (木花咲耶) is found at Asama Shrine on Mt. Fuji. The Nihon Shoki (日本書紀) also points to a wrestling match between Nomi no Sukune (野見宿禰) and Taima no Kehaya (当麻蹴), which is regarded today as the origin of Sumo. Hence the still valid idea that he is the protector of Sumo.

Suinin was the third prince of Emperor Sujin (崇神天皇) and Mimaki Hime (御間城姫).

His tomb is located at No. 11 Amagatsuji Nishimachi in Nara.

武内宿禰: Takeuchi no Sukune

Take no uchi no Sukune (武内宿禰) theoretically lived between 84 and 367: according to legend, he drank water from a secret well that served as an elixir of long life.

He is said to be the ancestor of the Soga clan (蘇我氏) and the Takeuchi clan (竹内氏), as well as 26 other clans. Emperors Ōjin (応神天皇) and Kōgen (孝元天皇) were also from the Takeuchi clan.

He served a total of 6 emperors: Keikō (景行天皇), Seimu (成務天皇), Chūai (仲哀天皇), Ōjin (応神天皇), Nintoku (仁徳天皇) and Empress Regent Jingū (神功皇后).

It was especially during Empress Jingū's reign that he was recognized as Grand Minister because he would accompany her to conquer part of Korea.

He would be accused of treason by Emperor Ōjin. This was all the work of his brother, Umashiuchi no Sukune (甘美内宿禰), who falsely accused him of plotting against imperial power to bring him down.

Both brothers were forced to bathe in boiling water to discover the truth: Takeuchi was cleared of suspicion and his brother was found guilty. It is said that those who lied in this bath would suffer burns from the punishment of the gods. This kind of ancestral trial is called "Kukatachi" (盟神探湯).

抓津姫命: Tsumatsu Hime no Mikoto

Daughter of Susanoo (素戔嗚命), she is a tree deity. She is the younger sister of two forest-related deities: the god Isotakeru no Kami (五十猛神) and the goddess Ōyatsu Hime

(大屋津姫命). She travels all over the country to scatter seeds that will become trees.

綱長井神: Tsunagai no Kami

Tsunagai no Kami is one of the 5 deities known under the generic name of Ikasuri no Mikannagi no Matsuru Kami (坐摩巫祭), organized by the Department of Shintō Affairs (Jingi-kan - 神祇官) in the 7th century AD. The five gods are:

- Ikuwi no Kami (生井神): protector of life

- Sakuwi no Kami (福井神): bringer of good fortune

- Tsunagawi no Kami (綱長井神): luck-bringer when fishing

- Hahiki no Kami (波比祇神): protector of the home and garden

- Asuha no Kami (阿須波神): protector of walkers and travelers

This is a deity related to fishing, who is worshipped in the hope of catching large numbers of fish. The word Tsunagai refers to the fact that a small fishing boat was sent to the end of a long rope at the bottom of a well. This divine homage made it possible to have a deep, pure and clean well. Tsunagai no Kami is thus by extension a water deity.

産土大神: Ubusuna no Ōkami

Ubusuna protects people and the land.

He protects the individual from before birth until death. Contrary to many of the mystics, here we are dealing with a deity that is older and closer to the early animism of Shintoism. We speak then of a natural deity.

While clans establish bonds through blood, this god strengthens communities that create bonds through geographic proximity. This is especially true in cities: the group of individuals feels a sense of faith in a local bond rather than pure genetics.

Some shrines are then linked to birth and especially childbirth. This relationship between birthplace and geographical proximity causes the development of folk customs, rituals, and festivals. This is why Ubusuna no Ōkami is also gradually being regarded as a deity of childbirth.

With time and history, beliefs in these deities tend to disappear as they are absorbed by others.

宇摩志阿斯訶備比古遅神: Umashiashikabi Hiko Ji no Kami

Appearing after the first 3 deities, grouped under the name Kotoamatsukami (別天神) at the time of the creation of the Earth and the

Heavens (Tenchikaibyaku - 天地開闢), he represents Energy and vitality.

Its name indicates several elements that symbolize the life force:

- Umashi: something good, something positive.

- Ashi: the reed

- Kabi: something that germinates or ferments (in essence, lives and dies).

In other words, he is a god who represents the life force symbolized by the shoots of the reeds.

宇志比古命: Ushi Hiko no Mikoto

He is usually found under the name Tanba Michinushi no Mikoto (丹波道主命). He is mainly referred to for advising Emperor Sujin (崇神天皇). He is said to be the son of Hikoimasu (彦坐王) and the great-grandson of

Emperor Kaika (開化天皇). Other sources indicate that he is actually the son of another son of Emperor Kaika, Hikoyusumi no Mikoto (彦湯産隅命).

Ushi Hiko is said to have formed the Shidō shōgun (四道将軍) with 3 other commanders sent by Emperor Sujin to pacify various regions:

- Ōbiko no Mikoto was sent to the North (Hokurikudō)

- Takenunakawake no Mikoto to the East (Tokaidō)

- Kibitsuhiko no Mikoto in the West (San'yōdō)

- Tanba no Michi no Ushi no Mikoto in the South (Tanba province).

Legend says they would return after 6 months, triumphant. This period allowed the power of the imperial family to assert itself in Yamato.

There is still some doubt that it was Ushi Hiko who went to the South; the Kojiki (古事記) indicates that it was his father Hikoimasu (彦坐王).

The Imperial Agency (宮内庁) does not consider Ushi Hiko buried in a particular mausoleum. However, it is common to think that he is at Kumobu Kurumazuka Mausoleum (雲部車塚古墳) in Higashihonjo, Tamba-Sasayama, Hyogo Prefecture.

表筒男命: Uwatsutsu no Ono Mikoto

Uwatsutsu no Ono Mikoto is the god of surface water currents.

He is one of the three deities of Sumiyoshi (住吉). This divine trinity protects humans who navigate the seas and oceans. They are also known to be the deities of trade. Ki no Tsurayuki, author of Tosa Nikki (土佐日記), indicates that they would be uncompromising when it comes to negotiation! Everything has a value, a price. When souls in distress offered goods to the gods to be saved from a storm, the gods waited for the unfortunates to offer them more beautiful offerings, including a beautiful mirror. The sea calmed and the surface became as flat and bright as the offered mirror.

Izanagi returned from the underworld covered in dirt and felt the need to wash himself. It was then, in the midst of the current in which the co-creator God of the world was purifying himself, that Uwatsutsu would be born.

Sumiyoshi's 3 deities appeared at the same time as the 3 sea dragons called Watatsumi Sanjin (綿津見三神), legendary dragons of the 3 water levels (high, medium and low) of a sea. Originally, each Sumiyoshi god was one of the 3 Watatsumi. They would represent the constellation Orion, once used to guide sailors in the dead of night.

Â-日女尊: Wakahirume no Mikoto.

Wakahiru Mikoto is a goddess recognized as a deity of the Ikuta Shrine (生田神社), mentioned in the Kojiki (古事記). Her name would mean "the young and innocent sun goddess."

When Susanoo (素戔嗚命) was in Takama ga Hara (高天原 - the Plain of Heaven where the heavenly gods live), she saw Wakahirume. While she was weaving a sacred robe in Amaterasu's workshop (天照), he broke the roof and threw a flayed horse into the room. The animal fell as fast as a meteorite. Wakahirume was badly wounded and died from his injuries.

Following this event, Amaterasu (天照) took refuge in the Amano-Iwato cave (天岩戸).

Wakahirume no Mikoto is thought to be a younger sister of the goddess Amaterasu (天照), or at least a deity very close to her.

One might also think that Wakahirume is the representation of Amaterasu (天照) herself, before the event. This coincides with the fact that Susanoo (素戔嗚命) always wanted to please her sister. In fact, Susanoo (素戔嗚命) can be regarded as an untamed child who attracts attention by doing stupid things. By throwing a horse into his sister's workshop, he represents a rascal who wants to play with his busy sister so badly that he breaks her toys (here the workshop, which can also be represented as the bubble of childhood bursting). When enough is enough, the innocent young girl (Wakahirume) goes into a black rage and breaks ties with her brother. The young girl gains character and becomes an adult: Amaterasu (天照). While Wakahirume represents kindness, Amaterasu (天照) is more imposing and fearsome. Emperors themselves avoid going to Ise's shrine to worship her for fear of her power.

雅武彦命: Wakatake Hiko no Mikoto

The son of Emperor Kōrei (孝霊天皇) and Haeiroto (絚某弟), he is the half-brother of Kibitsu Hiko no Mikoto (吉備津彦命).

A legend indicates that he would follow Kibitsu Hiko no Mikoto to put an end to the demon Ura (温羅) that terrorized the provinces of Sanuki (讃岐国) and Kibi (吉備国).

Together with his half-brother, they are the ones who inspired the folk tale of Momotarō (桃太郎), this young boy seeking wealth in the land of demons.

八柱御子命: Yahashira no Mikogami no Mikoto

It is a deity grouping 8 major astral deities in Buddhism. They are the gods of the 8 directions.

Following the mixture of Buddhism and Shintoism (which is called Shinbutsu shūgō - 神仏習合), the zodiac deities were mixed with:

- Taisaishin (太歳神): an astral mind of Jupiter, responsible for vegetation during the 4 seasons,

- Daishōgun (大将軍): an astral spirit of Venus, great general and king of the sky,

- Taionjin (太陰神): an astral spirit of Saturn, deity of arts and knowledge,

- Saigyōshin (歳刑神): an astral spirit of Mercury, deity of retributive justice,

- Saihashin (歳破神): an astral spirit of Saturn, the deity of earth from earth,

- Saisetsushin (歳殺神): an astral spirit from Mars, guardian of warriors and samurai,

- Ōbanshin (黄幡神): an astral spirit of the eclipse, guardian of the foundation of villages,

- Hyoubishin (豹尾神): an astral mind representing the Three Jewels (三宝) of Buddhism.

倭姫命: Yamato Hime no Mikoto

Yamato Hime is the fourth daughter of Emperor Suinin (垂仁天) and Hibasu Hime no Mikoto (日葉酢媛命).

According to the legend of the Nihon Shoki (日本書紀), about 2,000 years ago the emperor ordered his daughter Yamato Hime no Mikoto (倭比売命) to find a permanent place to worship the goddess Amaterasu (天照). After 20 years of searching for the best place, he had the inner shrine of Ise (Naiku) built at the request of the goddess. It was led by Izawatomi no Mikoto (伊佐波登美命).

She is also said to be the direct origin of Saigu (斎王) and Itsuki no Miko (斎皇女), that is, the celibate imperial priestesses of Ise Shrine and Kamo Shrine (賀茂神社).

倭大国魂神: Yamato no Ōkunitama no Kami

This god represents both the power of the Empire and the true Ruler of the Empire.

It is indicated in the Nihon Shoki (日本書紀) that a cult would be dedicated to him from the 6th year of Emperor Sujin's reign (崇神天皇). This was also the case with the goddess Amaterasu.

These two deities were then regarded as the creator of the Japanese Empire and as the Sun Goddess who watches over the Japanese Empire. Out of fear of their power, the emperor preferred to move the place of worship from inside the imperial palace to outside.

Emperor Sujin (崇神天皇) decided to divide the worship of these gods into 2. His 2 daughters are then in charge of the rites:

- The imperial family on the side of Toyosukiiri Hime no Mikoto (豊鍬入姫命) would worship the goddess Amaterasu (天照).

- The imperial family on the side of Nunakijo Iri Bime no Mikoto (渟名城入姫命) would worship the god Yamato no Ōkunitama.

日本武尊: Yamato Takeru no Mikoto

He would be the second or third prince of Emperor Keikō (景行天皇), and his mother was Harima no Inabi no Ōiratsume (播磨稲日大郎姫), according to the Sendaikuji Hongi (先代旧事本紀) and the Kojiki (古事記).

He would have been the father of the 14th emperor, Chūai (仲哀天皇).

There are several explanations regarding his name "Takeru." The first, and explained in the Kojiki (古事記), is that he is the one who rules the territory "Yamato" (日本 - name given to Japan at that time). The second is that "Takeru" is a word that expresses barbarism, opposing the nobility of an imperial family. He is said to have killed his brother Ōsu no Mikoto (小碓命) after tearing off every limb of his body. This would coincide with the fact that Emperor Keikō suspected Yamato Takeru. The Nihon Shoki (日本書紀) brings a warlike view of the character, while the Kojiki (古事記) tends to touch the reader's heart by showing a more dramatic character.

For the warrior version, it is said that after defeating the Kumaso (熊襲 - people of southern Kyūshū), Yamato Takeru killed the gods Ana no Watari no Kami (吉備の穴済の神) and Kashiwa no Watari no Kami (難波の柏済の神) in order to open a path between the water and the land and then receive praise from his father.

When he went to Sagami Province (相模国), now Kanagawa Prefecture, Yamato Takeru fell into a trap. His enemies attacked him and set fire to the grass near him. He opened his bag and retrieved a flint his aunt had given him. Yamato Takeru used the sword Kusanagi no Tsurugi (天叢雲剣 - also called a "grass cutter") to cut the grass and prepare an ambush. He surrounded himself with straw, burned it himself with flint, and protected himself from his enemy's attack with his own fire barrier. His stratagem then enabled him to escape, while his opponents waited for him on foot.

Once, while he was conquering an area, he faced 8 Tsuchigumo (土蜘蛛 - spider from Japanese folklore actually corresponding here to a traitor clan) in Yatsuki (八槻 - Fukushima prefecture). Yamato Takeru shot 8 arrows that sounded like thunder. 7 Tsuchigumo fled and gave up attacking him, while the eighth Tsuchigumo died instantly. Out of the spider came a sprout, which resulted in a beautiful Zelkova (Keyaki - 欅) tree.

Passing a beautiful girl along the river, he asked her for directions. She made him think she was deaf so she would not answer him. Later, after his expedition to the East, Yamato Takeru went to Owari to find a wife there on divine guidance. She was Miyazu Hime, the young woman by the river.

They married and, it is said, consummated the marriage through a moon veil.

He is said to have left her the sword after learning that there was an angry deity on Mount Ibuki (伊吹山) in the ancient province of Ōmi (近江国 - present-day Shiga Prefecture). He wanted to get rid of it with his bare hands, and when he got there, a god blocked his way. Thinking that it was not what he was looking for, the god turned into a huge snake (or a giant white boar, depending on the version). It threw ice on Yamato Takeru and he lost his way until he passed out. He managed to find his way back down the mountain and arrived near a water source. Fate came upon him and he became seriously ill as a result of this misadventure. Wanting to go to Ise, he made a detour to Owari to find his companion and his sword. His strength was running out. He died after writing to his wife to watch over his sword.

Miyazu Hime built the Atsuta Shrine-jingū (熱田神宮) to protect her late husband's sword.

Legend says that Yamato Takeru turned into a swan at the Ōtori shrine (大鳥大社) to join Amaterasu (天照) in heaven.

Yamato Takeru is described as a tragic hero in Kojiki (古事記), one of the most endearing stories in the book. It is said that he knew his power and knew that it would lead him to accomplish remarkable military feats. Yamato Takeru was loyal to his emperor. He embarked on conquests in both the West and the East, impelled by the blessing of Amaterasu (天照).

The Sun Goddess gave him the legendary sword of Susanoo (素戔嗚命), Kusanagi no Tsurugi (草薙の剣) to defeat his enemies. Today he is more than a hero; he is a deity.

3 mausoleums are dedicated to him throughout Japan:

- The Nobono no Haka (能褒野墓) in Kameyama (亀山市), Mie Prefecture.

- The Shiratori no Misasagi (白鳥陵) in Habikino (羽曳野市), Osaka Prefecture.

- The Shiratori no Misasagi (白鳥陵) in Gose (御所市), Nara Prefecture

八坂刀売神: Yasakatome no Kami

Yasakatome is the wife of Takeminakata no Kami (建御名方神), said to be flourishing.

According to the Kawai Shrine (川合神社), she and her husband are said to have drained water from the Kamiminochi Mountains (上水内郡) and dumped it into the Sea of Japan. Thanks to them, the land was finally leveled and crops began to grow.

One legend says that they put a ball of hot water on the ground and hot water gushed out of the earth. This is how the Suwa Onsen Hot Springs (諏訪温泉) appeared. It is said that if a person with an impure spirit enters this hot water, then the water becomes muddy.

## 用明天皇: Yōmei Tennō

Emperor Yōmei (Unknown - May 21, 587) was the 31st emperor of Japan . He reigned from September 5, 585 to April 9, 587.

He was the fourth son of Emperor Kinmei (欽明天皇). His mother was Soga no Kitashi Hime (蘇我堅塩媛), daughter of Soga no Iname (蘇我稲目). He is the father of Prince Shōtoku Taishi (聖徳太子).

He came to power upon the death of his brother, Emperor Bidatsu (敏達天皇). His reign did not really change the course of history, although he contributed to the controversial development of Buddhism in Japan. Emperor Yōmei was an ardent follower of the Buddha's teachings.

His mausoleum is located at Kasuga (Taishi) in Osaka's Minamikawachi district.

雄略天皇: Yūryaku Tennō

Yūryaku (age 418 - September 8, 479) was the 21st emperor of Japan. He reigned from December 25, 456 until his death. In the Kojiki (古事記), he is called Ōhatsuse no Ou (大長谷王), a rather exceptional name because the kanji of god (神) is usually used instead of the kanji of king (王).

He is the fifth son of Emperor Ingyō (允恭天皇) and Oshisaka no Ōnakatsu no Hime (忍坂大中姫).

Greedy for power, he fights against his brothers to become emperor upon the death of

Ankō (安康天皇) who was assassinated by Prince Mayowa (眉輪王). To avoid seeing another take power, he is also behind the death of Ichinohe no Oshiwa no Miko (市辺押磐皇子) who was to become the new emperor of Japan.

He was a powerful tyrant, ready to do anything to crush rebel forces in his way. He was said to be bloodthirsty and violent, capable of anything to achieve his ends or to proclaim his own justice.

He did not hesitate to murder people in his own family or to organize the murder of members of powerful families. His misdeeds led him to be called an evil emperor within his own territory. He was referred to as Hanahada Ashiki Tennō (大悪天皇), the emperor of heaven with immense cruelty.

With Yūryaku, Japan at the time went from an organization with several large clans to a centralized power around the emperor.

## Conclusion

We have come to the end of this journey. We have seen that Japanese mythology is important for several reasons.

It is true: every culture has its own legends, folk tales, and myths....

One of the reasons why Japanese mythology is still important is that it is pure storytelling.

It is also an excellent form of escapism -- something new, unique and different from what you are used to.

And I hope you found just that in this book.

Thank you for getting this far -- until the next adventure

www.ingramcontent.com/pod-product-compliance
Lightning Source LLC
Chambersburg PA
CBHW071450080526
44587CB00014B/2058